THE TRUTH ABOUT
PALESTINE

ISRAEL, THE BIBLE, AND
THE BATTLE FOR TRUTH

LARS ENARSON

ARIEL MEDIA   ARIELMEDIA.SHOP

Published by Ariel Media (*arielmedia.se*)
An imprint of The Watchman International, Inc. (*thewatchman.org*)
PO Box 94, Lake Mills, IA 50450, USA
Design: John Enarson

Previously published in Swedish as: *Sanningen om Palestina: Israel, Bibeln och striden om sanningen* (Sweden: Ariel Media, 2023).

First English Edition 2024
Printed in the United States of America
ISBN 979-8-9897241-0-9

For the truth

To Christi!

God bless you!

Ps 45:3-5

[signature]

CONTENTS

INTRODUCTION

This book deals with basic facts and background to the conflict around Palestine from a historical and biblical perspective. The conflict in the Middle East is primarily a battle for the truth. Unfortunately, media is more an actor than an observer in the story. There is, therefore, a great need to highlight facts that are often suppressed.

Overall, the conflict in the Middle East receives more media attention and more political involvement than any other event in the world. In the natural, this overrepresentation is completely absurd. We need spiritual eyes to be able to see what lies behind this anomaly. The current age is coming to an end and the birth pangs are not going to decrease—quite the opposite. The Middle East conflict affects us all, especially the Christian church, whether we like it or not.

Before taking a stand in this world conflict, we must examine its historical background and what the Scriptures have to say. It is crucial that we stand on the side of truth.

Chapter 1 examines Palestinian identity and what Palestinians themselves have said on the matter. It also highlights basic facts and common lies about Palestine and its history.

Chapter 2 asks whether a two-state solution is inevitable. Should the Holy Land be divided, and a new Palestinian state be created? Is land the main cause of the conflict?

Chapter 3 explores why the Jews are so hated? Why are they different and what is the reason behind the strong anti-Semitism present throughout history?

Chapter 4 deals with two widespread accusations against the Jewish people that are rarely analyzed: *The Protocols of the Elders of Zion* and its background, as well as the theory of Khazar Jews.

Chapter 5 highlights the spiritual dimension of the Palestine conflict. It is an end-time battle for the truth in which our love for the truth is decisive.

Chapter 6 discusses the biblical destiny of the Promised Land in salvation history, its future borders, and the so-called West Bank—Judea and Samaria.

Chapter 7 highlights Gaza's prophetic future, the role the conflict plays in Israel's spiritual restoration, and God's heart for the Arabs in, and around, Israel.

Appendix I addresses a question that is overwhelming and confusing to many: how can we as Christians pray in a war where people are killed?

Appendices II and III include critically important sources to be familiar with, from the constitutions of Hamas, the PLO, and Hezbollah, to the objectives of the Muslim Brotherhood.

May the Lord lead you as you read!

CHAPTER 1

ARE THE PALESTINIANS AN INVENTED PEOPLE?

"Take no part in the unfruitful works of darkness, but instead expose them." —Ephesians 5:11

Winston Churchill was one of the greatest statesmen of the 20th century. Boldly and purposefully, he fought until the end of World War II for the cause of freedom, against the despotism and cruelty of Nazism. He went against political correctness in the UK by proclaiming war against Hitler and Nazism.

Ronald Reagan was elected president of the United States in 1980. He did not hesitate to call communism by its true name: an evil empire[1] that needed to be defeated. He acted accordingly and towards

---

1   See Reagan's famous "Evil Empire" speech on March 8, 1983, "I urge you to beware of the temptation of pride—the temptation of blithely declaring yourselves above it all and label both sides equally at fault, to ignore the facts of history and the aggressive impulses of an evil empire, to simply call the arms race a giant misunderstanding and thereby remove yourself from the struggle between right and wrong and good and evil.

the end of his time in office, communism fell. One of Ronald Reagan's political advisors was Newt Gingrich. Much later, in the 2010s, Gingrich himself ran an election campaign to become president of the United States. He attracted a lot of attention through statements on the sensitive subject of Palestine. This is what he said in an interview:

> "Remember, there was no Palestine as a state. It was part of the Ottoman Empire until the early 20th century. I think that we've had an invented Palestinian people who are in fact Arabs, and who were historically part of the Arab community. And they had a chance to go many places, and for a variety of political reasons we have sustained this war against Israel now since the 1940s and it's tragic."[2]

Gingrich's clear statements resulted in an immediate reaction of furious condemnation from across the Arab world. But he refused to retract his statement. In a later debate, he clarified: "Is what I said factually true? Yes. Somebody ought to have the courage to tell the truth. ... It's fundamentally time for somebody to have the guts to stand up and say, 'Enough lying about the Middle East.'"[3] In another TV interview, he explained that the word "Palestinian" had not become a common term until after 1977. He continued: "This is a propaganda war in which our side refuses to engage and we refuse to tell the truth when the other side lies."[4]

---

2   Chana Ya'ar, "Gingrich: Barack 'Favoring the Terrorists,'" *Israel National News* (Dec 10, 2011), *https://israelnationalnews.com/news/150581#.Tu8-2GBuG2w* [Dec 22, 2023].

3   Tzvi Ben Gedalyahu, "Gingrich Says 'Enough Lying about the Middle East'", *Israel National News* (Dec 11, 2011), *https://israelnationalnews.com/news/150595 #.Tu869GBuG2w* [Dec 22, 2023].

4   Ibid.

It says of the antichrist, "and it will throw truth to the ground, and it will act and prosper." (Dan 8:12) The final battle will be a battle for the truth.

WHAT DO THEY THEMSELVES SAY?

What is the truth? Are the Palestinians an invented people? You don't have to trust Newt Gingrich's words on this. It is enough to quote what Palestinians and Arabs themselves have said.

Here are ten crystal clear statements from their own leaders:

1. The first statement comes from a congress of Muslim and Christian organizations in what was then Palestine, held in February 1919 to discuss the future of the area formerly ruled by the Ottoman Empire, which was dissolved after the First World War. The congress declared:

> **"We consider Palestine as part of Arab Syria as it has never been separated from it at any time. We are connected with it by national, religious, linguistic, moral, economic, and geographical bonds."[5]**

2. The Arab leader Auni Bey Abdul-Hadi said before the British Peel Commission in 1937:

> **"There is no such country as Palestine. 'Palestine' is a term the Zionists invented. There is no Palestine in the**

---

5   Michael Curtis, "Palestinians: Invented People", *BESA Center Perspectives Paper No. 157* (Dec 20, 2011, Begin–Sadat Center for Strategic Studies, Bar–Ilan University), *https://besacenter.org/palestinians-invented-people* [Dec 22, 2023].

Bible. Our country was for centuries part of Syria. 'Palestine' is alien to us. It is the Zionists who introduced it."[6]

3. The respected Arab scholar Philip Hittis testified before the Anglo-American Committee in 1946:

There has been no such thing as Palestine in history, "absolutely not."[7]

4. The Palestinian spokesman and Saudi Arabian ambassador to the UN, Ahmad Shuqeiri, told the UN Security Council in 1956:

"It is common knowledge that Palestine is nothing but Southern Syria."[8]

5. The PLO, in its own Charter or amended Basic Law (Article 1), states that,

"Palestine ... is an indivisible part of the Arab homeland, and the Palestinian people are an integral part of the Arab nation."[9]

---

6   Emmanuel Navon, "Tom, Gideon, Yossi and Amira", *Israel National News* (Dec 21, 2011), *https://israelnationalnews.com/news/339606#.TwSp4piXulI* [Dec 22, 2023].

7   Michael Curtis, "Palestinians" (2011).

8   Daniel Pinner, "Nakba: What's in a name?" *Jerusalem Post* (May 29, 2013), *https://jpost.com/opinion/op-ed-contributors/nakba-whats-in-a-name-314780* [Dec 22, 2023].

9   "The Palestinian National Charter: Resolutions of the Palestine National Council July 1–17, 1968", *The Avalon Project* (Yale Law School), *https://avalon.law.yale.edu/20th_century/plocov.asp* [Dec 22, 2023]

The "Arab homeland and... nation" today has 21 Arab states, but throughout history there has never been a state called Palestine.[10] (The equivalent of the letter "P" does not even exist in the Arabic alphabet or language.)

6. Zuheir Muhsein, then head of the PLO's military headquarters, said the following in an interview with the Dutch magazine *Trouw* in 1977:

> "The Palestinian people does not exist. The creation of a Palestinian state is only a means for continuing our struggle against the state of Israel for our Arab unity ... Only for political and tactical reasons do we speak today about the existence of a Palestinian people, since Arab national interests demand that we posit the existence of a distinct Palestinian people to oppose Zionism. For tactical reasons, Jordan, which is a sovereign state with defined borders, cannot raise claims to Haifa and Jaffa, while as a Palestinian, I can undoubtedly demand Haifa, Jaffa, Beer-Sheva and Jerusalem."[11]

7. At the Arab League meeting in Amman in November 1987, Jordan's king Hussein said:

> "The appearance of the Palestinian national personality comes as an answer to Israel's claim that Palestine is Jewish."[12]

---

10 Michael Curtis, "Palestinians" (2011).

11 James Dorsey, "Wij zijn alleen Palestijn om politieke reden", *Trouw* (March 31, 1977).

12 Martin Sherman, "UN-nation; un-nation; non-nation; anti-nation", *Jerusalem Post* (Sep 16, 2011), *https://jpost.com/opinion/columnists/un-nation-un-nation-non-nation-anti-nation* [Dec 22, 2023].

8. Israeli Arab Knesset Member, Azmi Bishara, gave a speech in 1994, in which he stated:

> "I think there is an Arab nation. I do not think there is a Palestinian nation. I think it's a colonialist invention ... When were there any Palestinians? ... until the 19th century Palestine was the south of greater Syria."[13]

9. Fathi Hammad, Hamas' Minister of Interior and Minister of National Security, announced on Egyptian TV "Al-Hekma" on March 23, 2012:

> "When we call for your help, it is with the aim of continuing the jihad. Praise Allah—all of us have Arab roots, and every Palestinian in the Gaza Strip and throughout Palestine is able to prove his Arab roots, whether from Saudi Arabia, Yemen, or anywhere else. We have blood ties ... Personally, half of my family is from Egypt. Where is your mercy? More than 30 families in the Gaza Strip are called Al-Masri [Egyptian]. Brothers, half of the Palestinians are Egyptians, and the other half are Saudis."[14]

10. The most prominent leader among the Palestinians was Yasser Arafat (1929–2004). Throughout his authorized biography by Alan Hart (*Arafat: Terrorist or Peacemaker?*), Arafat asserts at least a dozen times:

---

13 Martin Sherman, "Note to Newt (Part I): Uninventing Palestinians", *Jerusalem Post* (Dec 16, 2011), *https://jpost.com/opinion/columnists/note-to-newt-part-i-uninventing-palestinians* [Dec 22, 2023].

14 Nadav Shragai, "Palestinian nationhood? What does that mean", *Israel Hayom* (March 28, 2023), *https://www.israelhayom.com/2023/03/28/palestinian-nationhood-what-does-that-mean* [Dec 22, 2023].

"The Palestinian people have no national identity. I, Yasser Arafat, man of destiny, will give them that identity through conflict with Israel."[15]

All ten statements above, made by the Arabs' own leaders and spokesmen from 1919 until today, show that the Palestinian national identity is a very recent invention with no historical roots.

They also show that Palestinian identity is founded primarily on the attempt to destroy another state, instead of building its own.

ARAFAT

The Middle East conflict used to be described as an "Arab-Israeli conflict." It is, however, larger than the Arab world and can better be described as a Muslim conflict against Jewish independence, i.e. the many against the few. During the Cold War, the Soviet Union considered Israel to be too strong of an American influence in the Middle East. They therefore wanted to reframe the conflict into a large imperialistic Israel against a small opressed group.

Ion Mihai Pacepa was the highest-ranking intelligence officer ever to defect from the former Soviet Bloc. "Before I defected to America from Romania and left my post as manager for the Romanian intelligence service, I was responsible to give Arafat about $200,000 in laundered cash every month throughout the 1970s. I also sent two cargo planes each week to Beirut, filled with uniforms and supplies. Other Soviet Bloc states did similar."[16]

Yasser Arafat used to call himself a Palestinian refugee. However, he was born in Egypt in 1929, served in the Egyptian army and studied

---

15 Alan Hart, *Arafat: Terrorist or Peacemaker?* (London: Sidgwick and Jackson, 1984).

16 Ion Mihai Pacepa, "The KGB's Man", *Wall Street Journal* (Sep 22, 2003), *https://wsj.com/articles/SB106419296113226300* [Dec 22, 2023].

at Cairo University. Pacepa confirmed this in his revelations in *the Wall Street Journal,* 2003,

> "I received the KGB's 'personal file' on Arafat. He was an Egyptian citizen turned into a devoted Marxist by the KGB's foreign intelligence service. The KGB had trained him at its Balashikha special school east of Moscow and decided in the mid-1960s to mold him into the PLO's future leader. First, the KGB destroyed the official documents of Arafat's birth in Cairo and replaced them with fictitious documents stating that he had been born in Jerusalem and was therefore a Palestinian by birth ...

> "Arafat was an important agent of the KGB. Shortly after the Arab-Israeli Six Day War in 1967, Moscow appointed him chairman of the PLO. Egyptian leader Gamal Abdel Nasser, a Soviet puppet, proposed the appointment. 1969, KGB asked Arafat to proclaim war against the American 'imperialistic Zionism' ... It appealed to him so much that Arafat later claimed to have invented the 'imperialistic-Zionist' battle cry. But in fact 'imperialistic Zionism' was a Moscow invention, a modern adaptation of the *Protocols of the Elders of Zion*—long a favorite tool of Russian intelligence to stir up ethnic hatred. The KGB always considered anti-Semitism plus anti-imperialism as a rich source of anti-Americanism."[17]

Arafat managed to cause an incredible change. In less than 30 years, he created a Palestinian people and managed, with the help of

---

17   Ibid.

terrorist attacks,[18] to get the whole world to accept a special Palestinian people as if they had existed in the area since time immemorial.

THE NAME PALESTINE

Where does the name Palestine come from? The ancient Greek historian Herodotus once referred to the Gaza Strip inhabited by the ancient Philistines as a "district in Syria called Palaistine" (*Historia*, 5th century BC). A few times, the Hebrew Bible also describes the small coastal strip south of Jaffa as *pleshet*, i.e. the territory of the Philistines. But it was not a synonym for the Holy Land, which the local inhabitants called Israel, or Judah.

After the second Jewish revolt against Rome in 132–135, the Roman Emperor Hadrian forbade all Jews to remian in Jerusalem. At that time the province was called Judea. To try to wipe out the Jewish connection to the area, he gave the city of Jerusalem the Roman name Aelia Capitolina and renamed the country Syria-Palestine, to revive the memory of the Jews' worst historical enemies, the Philistines. (The ancient Philistines, a coastal people who originated from southeastern Europe, had long before disappeared as a distinct ethnic group.) The name change of Jerusalem did not last long. But the offensive name for the Holy Land, "Syria-Palestine," continued to live on in history, right up to 1948, especially in the Christian West. However, it was a foreign name to the Arab world, and internally the Jews throughout the ages consistently spoke of *Eretz Israel*—the Land of Israel.

---

18 Pacepa also mentions this side of Arafat, "I invented the hijackings [of passenger airplanes]', boasted Arafat when I first met him in his PLO headquarters in Beirut in the beginning of the 1970s. He made a gesture towards the small red flags on a wall map of the world (where Israel was 'Palestine'). 'There they all are!' he proudly declared" (*Wall Street Journal*, Sep 22, 2003).

7 TRUTHS ABOUT PALESTINE

The following are seven important historical truths about Palestine that are being ignored by politicians and the mass media today.

1. The first time that "Palestine" was officially named as a particular, defined geographical area came in connection with a decision by the League of Nations in the 1920s. It had to do with giving the British a "mandate" —the task—to restore to the Jewish people its independence by a state of their own in parts of the former Ottoman Empire—the British Mandate of Palestine.[19]

2. Ironically, before 1948, the word Palestinian was never used by the Arabs but only by the Jews in the area, such as in *the Palestine Post* (now *the Jerusalem Post*) and the Palestine Philharmonic Orchestra (now the Israel Philharmonic Orchestra). Only after the State of Israel was established in May 1948 did the word "Palestinian" begin to be used exclusively to refer to Arabs in the area."[20]

Former Israeli Prime Minister Golda Meir asked in an interview with British Thames television in 1970:

> "When were Palestinians born? What was all this area before the First World War when Britain got the mandate over Palestine? What was Palestine then? Palestine was then the area between the Mediterranean Sea and the Iraqi border. The East and West Banks were Palestine. I am Palestinian, from 1921 and 1948 I carried a Palestinian Passport. There existed nothing in this area such as 'Jews and Arabs and Palestinians'. There were Jews and Arabs."

3. The San Remo Conference 1920, where both Jews and Arabs were represented, assembled to decide the future of the Ottoman Empire after World War I. **This conference "recognized the Jewish peo-**

---

19 Michael Curtis, "Palestinians" (2011).

20 Ibid.

ple's historic rights to recreate their national home in Palestine." Pay close attention to the wording. No new rights were created, but only the **already existing historic rights** of the Jewish people to a national home in Palestine **were recognized.** This decision, by order of the League of Nations, made the Balfour Declaration binding according to international law. The San Remo Treaty, together with Article 22 of the League of Nations Convention and Article 80 of the UN Charter, still applies today. Forcing Israel to go back to the 1949 armistice lines (1967 "borders") and dividing Jerusalem is therefore a serious violation of international law.[21] This is also a reason why no country other than Great Britain and Pakistan recognized Jordan's annexation of the West Bank after 1948.

4. No independent Palestinian state has ever existed. Nor has there been a single administrative or cultural unit for Palestinians. The Arabs in the area were never in any way unlike other Arabs in the Middle East.[22]

5. One can read thousands of Arabic books and newspapers written before 1964, without finding anything about an Arabic or Muslim Palestinian state, or a reference to Arabs as uniquely Palestinians.[23]

6. There has never in the entire history of mankind, before the Jewish immigration began, existed any Palestinian king, sultan or monarch, no Palestinian capital in Jerusalem, no Palestinian poet, writer or intellectual who promoted a specific Palestinian culture. And there has never existed any Palestinian language.

7. The Jewish people did not get their country back from Arabs (or "Palestinians"), but first from the Turkish Empire and then from Great Britain. The Arabs had no sovereignty in the area, the

---

21 "Give Peace a Chance", *European Coalition For Israel* (2011), youtu.be/oVsjN-zXojCM [Dec 22, 2023].

22 Michael Curtis, "Palestinians" (2011).

23 Irwin Graulich, "Nu, Is Newt Right?" *Israel National News* (Dec 21, 2011), *https://israelnationalnews.com/news/339602#.TwQnzJiXulI* [Dec 22, 2023].

Turkish Ottoman Empire did. The frequent illustration based on various maps that show how the Palestinians gradually lost their own homeland is an example of a false history description, a distortion of history. The "Palestinians" have never owned "Palestine!"

In summary you can say that there never in history has existed any trace of an Arab Palestinian national identity, before the Jewish national endeavors began in the 20th century. Only after the formation of the state of Israel in 1948, and especially after the reunion of Jerusalem in 1967, the Arabs, with the help of the media, have successfully invented the current Palestinian identity. It is because of this that Newt Gingrich said,

> "The fact is, the Palestinian claim to a right of return is based on a historically false story. Somebody ought to have the courage to go all the way back to the 1921 League of Nations mandate for a Jewish homeland, and point out the context in which Israel came into existence. 'Palestinian' did not become a common term until after 1977. This is a propaganda war in which our side refuses to engage. And we refuse to tell the truth when the other side lies. And you're not gonna win the long run if you're afraid to stand firm and stand for the truth."[24]

However, the propaganda war has been successfully waged by the Palestine Liberation Organization (PLO) since it was founded by the KGB in 1964.

> "In 1948, Palestine meant a homeland for Jews. In 2011, Palestine means an oppressed, occupied, homeless Arab refugee subgroup being subjugated by those same Jews. What a brilliant marketing ploy. And when you couple the brand with other powerful buzzwords like Apartheid, Nazi-like,

---

24 David Singer, "Palestine: Time to Tell the Truth" (2011).

abuse, mistreat, persecute, conquer, etc., you create a powerful circumstance for undeserved compassion."[25]

5 OFT-REPEATED LIES ABOUT PALESTINE

If you base your story on lies, then you have to continue to build it on lies. Here are some of the historical, geographic, religious, and national lies that the "Palestinians" officially promote in their constitution, education, and media to bolster their Palestinian "identity."

1. **"The Jewish people have no historical background whatsoever in Palestine."** This claim makes most of the Bible a complete lie, not to mention all accepted, official historical, geographical and religious research. Most of the names of places in Judea and Samaria have a Hebrew origin, not Arabic.

2. **"The Jewish people are not a people, but only a religion. They therefore have no right to a country of their own, especially not in Palestine."** This false statement makes the God of the Bible a liar. The Jewish people is the only of all the peoples of the world whom God expressly calls His own chosen people. "For you are a people holy to the LORD your God. The LORD your God has chosen you to be a people for his treasured possession, out of all the peoples who are on the face of the earth." (Deut 7:6) "Israel," **both** as a people and a country, appears about 2,300 times in the Bible.

God's promise to give the land of Canaan to the descendants of Abraham, Isaac and Jacob as an eternal inheritance is the most repeated promise in the whole Bible!

> "He is the LORD our God; his judgments are in all the earth. He remembers his covenant forever, the word that he commanded, for a thousand generations, the covenant that he made with Abraham, his sworn promise to Isaac, which he

---

25 Irwin Graulich, "Nu, Is Newt Right?" (2011).

confirmed to Jacob as a statute, to Israel as an everlasting covenant, saying, 'To you I will give the land of Canaan as your portion for an inheritance.'" (Ps 105:7-11)

3. **"Jesus was a Palestinian, born of Palestinian parents. The virgin Mary was a Palestinian, and Jesus was the first Palestinian martyr."**[26] These false claims make the Gospel a complete lie. The New Testament opens with the words, "The book of the genealogy of Jesus Christ, the son of David, the son of Abraham." (Matt 1:1) and ends: "I, Jesus, have sent my angel to testify to you about these things for the churches. I am the root and the descendant of David, the bright morning star." (Rev 22:16) You can't be more Jewish than to be son to David and Abraham. Paul, the apostle to the Gentiles, wrote, "Remember Jesus Christ, risen from the dead, the offspring of David, as preached in my gospel." (2 Tim 2:8)

4. **"There have never been any Jewish temples on the Temple Mount in Jerusalem."** This statement means that not only are both the Old and New Testaments false documents, but also our Master and Savior was a liar when he spoke of the Jewish Temple in Jerusalem and called it his Father's house. In addition, this makes archaeological science a big lie. The area around the Temple Mount is one of the most excavated archaeological sites in the world. All professional archaeologists who have excavated there for the last hundred years have then been completely deceived.

5. **"The Palestinians are descendants of the ancient Philistines and Jebusites. They are as part of the Arab nation, a Semitic people in direct descent from Abraham through Ishmael."** Yassir Arafat used to say that as an Arab and therefore a Semite, he could not by definition be anti-Semitic. All these contradictory claims make both the Bible and accepted historical and ethnological research a lie. The Jebusites, like the Philistines, were non-Semitic people descended

---

26   Itamar Marcus, "Who was the Palestinian Jesus?" *Palestinian Media Watch* (Dec 24, 2020), *https://palwatch.org/page/18444* [Dec 22, 2023].

from Ham (Gen 10:14). Both disappeared from history long before the Common Era began.

These are just some of the lies. There are many others. For the "Palestinians" anything is fair game if it deprives the Jewish people of their heritage. And if you repeat lies enough times, most people end up believing them. The Nazis proved that this method works. If you then also impose the lies through violence, threats, and bloody terrorist acts, it works even better.

GOD'S FAITHFULNESS TOWARDS ISRAEL

Despite centuries of persecution and exile, the Jewish people have been preserved as a people for 3,500 years. Why? Simply because they are based on an eternal, unconditional covenant made by the Creator of heaven and earth with Abraham, Isaac and Jacob (not Ishmael and not Esau!). There is no other explanation for this unique fact. This reality, which has no historical counterpart, gave rise to the legend about Frederick II of Prussia. The king asked his doctor if he could give a single evidence of the existence of God and got the answer: "The Jews, Your Majesty!"

As a people, throughout their long history, the Jews have always considered what later came to be known as Palestine as their homeland. Jeremiah prophesied 2600 years ago: "Hear the word of the Lord, O nations, and declare it in the coastlands far away; say, 'He who scattered Israel will gather him, and will keep him as a shepherd keeps his flock.'" (Jer 31:10)

The concept that Yassir Arafat successfully sold to the whole world was this: "Give Palestine to the Palestinians!" Who can argue with such a self-written claim? The only problem is that before 1948 that statement basically meant: Give Palestine to the Jews! The famous UN vote in 1947 was about dividing Palestine into a Jewish and an **Arab** state, not one Jewish and one "Palestinian" state. In 1947, such a proposal would have been incomprehensible. When the Jews finally got their state, they renamed it Israel instead of Palestine,[27] in line with their ancient heritage and the representation of the Bible.[28]

The Arabs eventually took over the name Palestine, made it their own brand, and then successfully sold their fabricated history to an ignorant world, to arouse its sympathy. But it is a false sympathy. The Arabs already have 22 nations, one of which is already a "Palestinian," Arab state called Jordan. Another Palestinian state, at the expense of the only Jewish state in the world in its own ancient homeland, is a clear violation of both basic human rights and international legislation from previously concluded agreements.

The driving force behind all these lies is the deep hatred of Jews that exists within Islam. There is a famous Muslim holy text that urges all Muslims to commit genocide on the Jewish people, an ancient *hadith* that reads: "The time [Day of Judgment] will not come until Muslims will fight the Jews (and kill them); until the Jews hide behind rocks and trees, which will cry: O Muslim! there is a Jew hiding behind me, come on and kill him!"[29] Many Muslims today preach and believe in these words in the same way that Christians believe in the Bible.

Lies have no future. They are built on quicksand. Daniel Pipes has said: "... the fact that this [Palestinian] identity is of such recent and expedient origins suggests that.... it could eventually come to an end, perhaps as quickly as it got started."[30]

---

27   Before the state of Israel was proclaimed May 14, 1948, no outsider knew what the new state would be called.

28   The New Testament, also calls the country Israel, never Palestine, see Matt 2:20–21.

29   Quote from Article 7 of the Hamas Charter, quoting an ancient *hadith* cited by Bukhari and Muslim, the authors of the two most authoritative and widely accepted collections of *hadith* (traditions of the Prophet).

30   Daniel Pipes, "America's shiny new Palestinian militia," *Jerusalem Post* (March 17, 2010), *https://jpost.com/Opinion/Columnists/Americas-shiny-new-Palestinian-militia* [Dec 22, 2023].

One thing is certain: You cannot accept the Palestinian myth and at the same time believe in the Bible. The two are mutually exclusive.

CHAPTER 2

IS A TWO-STATE SOLUTION INEVITABLE?

"For behold, in those days and at that time, when I restore the fortunes of Judah and Jerusalem, I will gather all the nations and bring them down to the Valley of Jehoshaphat. And I will enter into judgment with them there, on behalf of my people and my heritage Israel, because they have scattered them among the nations and have divided up my land." —Joel 3:1–2

The UN stipulates that the indigenous population of an area automatically have the right to the country where they live. History shows that the Jewish people have the historical right to the area between the Mediterranean Sea and the Jordan River as its own homeland. Except for some brief periods, Jews have lived in this land ever since the days of Joshua, 3,500 years ago. There are not many people in the world today that have such a documented history back in time.

In 1922, therefore, the entire international community, through the predecessor of the UN, the League of Nations, unanimously recognized the historical rights of the Jewish people to establish a national home in the entire area that was then called the Palestine Mandate. This area covered from the beginning also today's Jordan. However, in 1921, Great Britain divided the area and gave that part to the Saudi Arabian royal family, Hussein ibn Ali in Mecca, before the decision was taken in the League of Nations to give the entire area to the Jewish people as a national home.

"Palestine-Arabs" cannot show a history in the area similar to that of the Jewish people. In a British census in Jerusalem in 1860, for example, Jews constituted the largest ethnic group in the city, even before modern Zionism emerged as a political movement.

No Palestinian state formation has ever existed throughout history. In 1917, the British took over Palestine from the Turks, who had ruled the area for 400 years. Before that, the area had been governed from Baghdad, Damascus and Cairo. Even Islam's holy book, the Quran, acknowledges that God gave the Holy Land to the Jewish people (*The Quran*, 5:20–107, 17:104).

THE JEWS ARE NO FOREIGN COLONIZERS

The Jews are in other words no colonizers in Israel, that has deprived another people of their original homeland. That is a lie that communism launched. **At the time of Jesus two thousand years ago, people did not speak Arabic in the Holy Land. Hebrew and Aramaic were spoken.** The country was not called Palestine. It was called Israel just as it is today. Matthew writes about this,

> "But when Herod died, behold, **an angel of the Lord** appeared in a dream to Joseph in Egypt, saying, 'Rise, take the child and his mother and **go to the land of Israel**, for those who sought the child's life are dead.' And he rose and took the child and his mother and went to **the land of Israel**." (Matt 2:19–21)

Throughout history, there has never been a separate Arab, Palestinian, national identity before Zionism arose. There exists not a single known Palestinian-Arab leader throughout history before that, no separate Palestinian language and above all no Palestinian state. For 3,000 years, Jerusalem has never been the capital of any state other than a Jewish one. The only exception is the short period that the Crusaders counted Jerusalem as their capital. But this "Christian kingdom" did not constitute a nation in the classical sense.

The "Palestinians" consist primarily of immigrated Arabs. They have no more rights to a country of their own than minorities in the United States have a right to their own country. There exists no historical reason for this. The Jewish people, on the other hand, have historical rights to the land. They are the only definable indigenous population in the area.

THE PRIMARY CAUSE OF THE CONFLICT

The reason why the "Palestinians" today demand their own state in addition to the one that already exists in Jordan, is primarily due to Islam's built-in hatred of Jews. The Palestinian terrorists are not shouting "For Palestine!" when they murder Jews today in Israel or in other parts of the world. They shout out the Muslim creed *"Allah hu akbar!"* which means "god is great" or "god is greater." They are motivated to wipe out Israel and to carry out terrorist attacks and murder all Jews based on the teachings of Islam and the Imams' promise that they will get to enjoy 72 virgins in paradise if they commit these terrorist acts.

The Palestinian national movement is from its inception a racist, anti-Semitic, genocidal project built on lies. The world has been seduced into embracing this lie with the help of the Arab oil weapon combined with atheistic left-wing propaganda.

There are no Arabs in the Middle East who have greater democratic rights and freedoms than what the Arabs in Israel have. Israel is a blessing for both Arabs and Jews. Jerusalem Post columnist Caroline

Glick shows this clearly in her pioneering book, *The Israeli Solution: A One-State Plan for Peace in the Middle East.*[31] A two-state solution would not only affect the Arabs negatively. It would in the end mean the downfall of both Europe and America if developments continue as they are now. "First the Saturday people, then the Sunday people!" is the saying of the Islamists.

Those who more than any others support and encourage the Palestinian terrorists today are the EU. The extermination of six million Jews in Europe did not occur in a vacuum. Anti-Semitism has been a deep-rooted part of European culture for centuries and today, only one generation after the Holocaust, they have opened wide their arms to Islam's fanatical Jew-hatred and abandoned Israel.

During the Middle Ages, the Jews in Europe were persecuted for their religion. After the Enlightenment, it was no longer possible to persecute someone for religious reasons, so anti-Semitism changed its shape and instead began to persecute the Jews for their race. After the Holocaust it is no longer possible to persecute someone because of race, so now the Jews are persecuted both in Europe and around the world for their state. Hatred of Israel is the anti-Semitism of our time.

The Palestinian two-state project has, from its inception, been a racist genocidal project. Its founder Sheik Amin al-Husseini, who was Yasser Arafat's predecessor, called on all Arabs to kill the Jews immediately after the San Remo decision in 1920. Along with Adolf Hitler, he planned the extermination of the Jews in Palestine during the Second World War. This genocidal project was then carried on by the modern godfather of international terrorism, Yassir Arafat, and Palestine is today the special foster child of radical Islam. "*Itbach el Yahud!,*" "Kill the Jews!" is an Arab slogan that has sounded for centuries in the Middle East, ever since the days of Muhammad. This bloody appeal to genocide that has been practiced several times earlier in

---

31 Caroline Glick, *The Israeli Solution: A One-State Plan for Peace in the Middle East* (New York: Crown Forum, 2014).

history, is today undergoing an eerie renaissance throughout the Muslim world.

Through terrorist threats and by using the access to Arabic oil as blackmail, the entire international community has in less than 100 years changed its mind and decided that the problems in the Middle East must be solved through the so-called two-state solution: the formation of a Palestinian state alongside an Israeli state in the Holy Land. When the Messiah comes, he will judge the whole world for dividing up God's own land in this way.

> "For behold, in those days and at that time, when I restore the fortunes of Judah and Jerusalem, I will gather all the nations and bring them down to the Valley of Jehoshaphat. And **I will enter into judgment with them there**, on behalf of my people and my heritage Israel, because they have scattered them among the nations and **have divided up my land**." (Joel 3:1–2)

In recent years, however, faith in the two-state solution has begun to falter and an increasing number of people now speak more or less openly about the necessity that the state of Israel must cease to exist, and be replaced by an altogether Palestinian state. The formation of a Palestinian state through the so-called two-state solution constitutes the largest threat against Israel's existence, even worse than a nuclear-armed Iran. The pressure from the outside world on Israel to accept this suicidal project is enormous.

IS A PALESTINIAN STATE INEVITABLE?

Some object that if the Messiah will judge all the nations of the world for dividing up God's own land, there is nothing we can do about it. It must happen according to the prophetic word.

To this we may object that although a Palestinian state does not yet exist in practice, Joel's prophecy has already been fulfilled. The whole world has already divided the land of Israel. The United Nations has recognized Palestine as a state with observer status in the UN and have included Palestine in a large amounts of its organs. However, the decision of the international community has not yet succeeded in being implemented in Israel in a purely practical sense.

The LORD has promised to make Jerusalem a heavy stone for all peoples and that anyone who tries to lift it will be hurt.

"On that day I will make Jerusalem a heavy stone for all the peoples. All who lift it will surely hurt themselves. And all the nations of the earth will gather against it." (Zec 12:3)

Psalm 2 is about the rebellion of the nations against God regarding Jerusalem. God declares how he reacts to this: "He who sits in the heavens laughs; the Lord holds them in derision. Then he will speak to them in his wrath and terrify them in his fury, saying, 'As for me, I have set my King on Zion, my holy hill.'" (Ps 2:4–6) The two-state solution includes a division of Jerusalem where the Temple Mount, God's holy Mount Zion, would be taken from Israel. We are called to warn the nations of the world about this. Verse 10 says: "Now therefore, O kings, be wise; be warned, O rulers of the earth!"

> "Let all the earth fear the Lord; let all the inhabitants of the world stand in awe of him! For he spoke, and it came to be; he commanded, and it stood firm. The Lord brings the counsel of the nations to nothing; **he frustrates the plans of the peoples.** The counsel of the Lord stands forever, the plans of his heart to all generations." (Ps 33:8–11)

This means that it will not be easy for anyone, including the White House and the UN, to divide the Land of Israel. The LORD will frustrate the plans that go against His plans for Jerusalem. God's holy Name will be glorified in the end times, as He continues to restore Israel, despite the opposition of the whole world. The glorification of God's Name is the main reason why we should pray that God prevents the international community's plan to implement a two-state solution!

The LORD wants instead to glorify His holy name throughout the earth by expanding Israel's borders! "But you have increased the nation, O Lord, you have increased the nation; you are glorified; you have enlarged all the borders of the land." (Isa 26:15)

The Messiah taught us how to pray. He said: "You shall pray like this: Our Father in heaven, let your name be glorified. Let your kingdom come. Let your will happen, on the earth as in heaven" (Matt 6:9-10 Svenska Folkbibeln 2015, translated). The LORD has promised:

> "Hear the word of the Lord, O nations, and declare it in the coastlands far away; say, 'He who scattered Israel will gather him, and will keep him as a shepherd keeps his flock.' ... And it shall come to pass that as I have watched over them to pluck up and break down, to overthrow, destroy, and bring harm, so I will watch over them to build and to plant, declares the Lord." (Jer 31:10, 28)

THE PROPHETIC MINISTRY OF HAGGAI AND ZECHARIAH

There is a remarkable parallel in the Word of God to what is happening right now in Israel. When the Jews returned from Babylon, it was through a decree from the Persian king Koresh.

> "In the first year of Cyrus king of Persia, that the word of the Lord by the mouth of Jeremiah might be fulfilled, the Lord stirred up the spirit of Cyrus king of Persia, so that he made a proclamation throughout all his kingdom and also put it in writing: 'Thus says Cyrus king of Persia: The Lord, the God of heaven, has given me all the kingdoms of the earth, and he has charged me to build him a house at

Jerusalem, which is in Judah. Whoever is among you of all his people, may his God be with him, and let him go up to Jerusalem, which is in Judah, and rebuild the house of the Lord, the God of Israel—he is the God who is in Jerusalem. And let each survivor, in whatever place he sojourns, be assisted by the men of his place with silver and gold, with goods and with beasts, besides freewill offerings for the house of God that is in Jerusalem.'" (Ezra 1:1–4)

Koresh's decree is similar to the decision made by the League of Nations in 1922, when it gave Great Britain the task of implementing the Balfour Declaration by giving the Jewish people a national home in Palestine.

After Koresh's decision to give the Jewish people freedom to return and restore the Temple in Jerusalem, there was opposition from the neighboring peoples all around. The opposers first wanted to help build the Temple, but when they were not allowed, they became aggressive. "Then the people of the land discouraged the people of Judah and made them afraid to build and bribed counselors against them to frustrate their purpose." (Ezra 4:4–5)

After a while, the neighboring people wrote a letter to the king in Persia where they on false grounds accused the Jews for being rebellious and that the restoration of Jerusalem would cause much harm. The king then wrote a reply in which he forced the Jews to stop rebuilding Jerusalem.

"Then, when the copy of King Artaxerxes' letter was read before Rehum and Shimshai the scribe and their associates, they went in haste to the Jews at Jerusalem and by force and power made them cease. Then the work on the house of God that is in Jerusalem stopped, and it ceased until the second year of the reign of Darius king of Persia." (Ezra 4:23–24)

It is exactly the same thing that has happened in our day in relation with the return of the Jewish people to their own land. They were first allowed to do this in 1922, but due to resistance from in particular the Muslims in the Middle East, Israel has been forced to give up the rights it received in 1922. The entire international community is now demanding that Israel give up part of its land—and most importantly, Jerusalem—to a Muslim, Palestinian state.

But the prophets Haggai and Zechariah encouraged the Jews to defy the new decision and continue to build on God's house in Jerusalem. "Now the prophets, Haggai and Zechariah the son of Iddo, prophesied to the Jews who were in Judah and Jerusalem, in the name of the God of Israel who was over them. Then Zerubbabel the son of Shealtiel and Jeshua the son of Jozadak arose and began to rebuild the house of God that is in Jerusalem, and the prophets of God were with them, supporting them." (Ezra 5:1–2)

When there were protests and King Darius demanded an explanation for the Jews defying the decree to stop building the Temple, the Jewish leaders gave the king the following answer:

"We are the servants of the God of heaven and earth, and we are rebuilding the house that was built many years ago, which a great king of Israel built and finished. But because our fathers had angered the God of heaven, he gave them into the hand of Nebuchadnezzar king of Babylon, the Chaldean, who destroyed this house and carried away the people to Babylonia. However, in the first year of Cyrus king of Babylon, Cyrus the king made a decree that this house of God should be rebuilt. And the gold and silver vessels of the house of God, which Nebuchadnezzar had taken out of the temple that was in Jerusalem and brought into the temple of Babylon, these Cyrus the king took out of the temple of Babylon, and they were delivered to one whose name was Sheshbazzar, whom he had made governor; and he said to him, 'Take these vessels, go and put them in the temple that is in Jerusalem, and let the house of God be re-built on its site.' Then this Sheshbazzar came and laid the foundations of the house of God that is in Jerusalem, and from that time until now it has been in building, and it is not yet finished. Therefore, if it seems good to the king, let search be made in the royal archives there in Babylon, to see whether a decree was issued by Cyrus the king for the rebuilding of this house of God in Jerusalem. And let the king send us his pleasure in this matter." (Ezra 5:11–17)

When Darius did research, Koresh's command was found and ac-knowledged that the Jews were right. He sent a response where he commanded that the work to establish the Temple should be sup-ported. The letter ended with these words: "May the God who has caused his name to dwell there overthrow any king or people who shall put out a hand to alter this, or to destroy this house of God that is in Jerusalem. I Darius make a decree; let it be done with all dili-gence." (Ezra 6:12)

Today we are called to act in the same way as the prophets Haggai and Zechariah did. We shall pray for and encourage the Jewish people to realize the Zionist vision of restoring Israel according to the pro-phetic word and the decision that was established by the internation-al community 1922.

The leaders of Israel need courage today to act in the same way as the Jewish leaders did after the return from Babel, by boldly claiming their divine, historical and legal rights to their own homeland in the entire area between the Jordan River and the Mediterranean Sea.

The two-state solution is not God's will. It will not solve the con-flict in the area and is a great danger for Israel. The Antichrist will ul-timately offer Israel some kind of false peace plan, but it will lead to the greatest existential threat to the Jewish people in its history.

We should today, in the same way as the prophets Haggai and Zechariah did in their time, encourage the Jewish people in their rights to the entire Land of Israel, although the international community now has changed its mind and demands that the Jews must vacate the areas where they have their strongest historical and religious roots.

THE PALESTINIANS ALREADY HAVE A STATE OF THEIR OWN

In the decision that was taken in the League of Nations 1922, the Jewish people were given the national rights in the entire area that was then called Palestine. The Arabs got national rights in Lebanon, Syria and Iraq. In the Palestine mandate, the Arabs were given civil and religious rights, but not national rights. No distinct "Palestinian" people existed at this time. It is a much later invention. Nor did any "Palestinian" people exist at the time of the UN vote in 1947 on dividing Palestine. The vote concerned a division of the country into a Jewish and an **Arab** state, not a "Palestinian" state.

"Palestinians" say themselves in the PLO charter that they constitute one part of the "Arab nation." The Arab nation today has 21 states within an area almost as large as the United States. All these states have the same language, the same dominant religion, and the same culture and consider themselves the "Arab nation."

The Arabs also already have an Arab, Palestinian state called Jordan. **After the San Remo decision in 1920, Great Britain cut off almost 80% of the Palestine mandate that was promised the Jews as a homeland and gave this area to the Arabs.** This then led in 1946 to the formation of the Palestinian Arab state of Transjordan, which today is called Jordan.

The solution to the conflict between Arabs and Jews in the Middle East is not to give the Arabs a 22nd state and the "Palestinian" Arabs another state, any more than the solution to the racial conflicts in the United States is to give minorities their own country in the United States. There is no serious politician who would propose such a solution.

The only feasible way to resolve the conflict between Jews and Arabs, is to work for a peaceful coexistence between them. **The Muslim, religious fanaticism and jihadism that incites to hatred and murder of Jews constitutes the largest obstacle for peace.** The problem is that today's politicians refuse to acknowledge this, and even more so, to deal with it.

THE ANTICHRIST'S PEACE PLAN

Antichrist will appear in the last days as a false messianic prince of peace. According to the book of Daniel, he will lure Israel into a false peace alliance during seven years, but the peace will not hold. Already after three and a half years it will be broken. It is not difficult to see the contours to this false peace by the entire world's pressure on Israel to recognize the so-called two-state solution. This is nothing but the enemy's plan to destroy Israel.

A two-state solution will not bring lasting peace, but will instead lead to a major military conflict, where the armies of the nations will perish as they try to wipe out Israel to create peace. "While people are saying, 'There is peace and security,' then sudden destruction will come upon them as labor pains come upon a pregnant woman, and they will not escape." (1 Thess 5:3)

The Messiah will intervene to save Israel. Isaiah prophesied about the plans of the nations against Jerusalem and how a military attack will lead to great disappointment. As it is written,

> "And the multitude of all the nations that fight against Ariel, all that fight against her and her stronghold and distress her, shall be like a dream, a vision of the night. As when a hungry man dreams, and behold, he is eating, and awakes with his hunger not satisfied, or as when a thirsty man dreams, and behold, he is drinking, and awakes faint, with his thirst not quenched, so shall the multitude of all the nations be that fight against Mount Zion." (Isa 29:7–8)

The prophet Zechariah describes in more detail how the battle against Jerusalem will lead to the arrival of the Messiah. "Behold, a day is coming for the Lord, when the spoil taken from you will be divided in your midst. For I will gather all the nations against Jerusalem to battle, and the city shall be taken and the houses plundered and the women raped. Half of the city shall go out into exile, but the rest of the people shall not be cut off from the city." (Zech 14:1–2)

This prophecy was partially fulfilled during Israel's War of Independence in 1948, when Jerusalem was divided, and the Jewish population of the Old City of Jerusalem was displaced by the Arab armies. But above all, there is a future fulfillment of the prophecy in connection with the arrival of the Messiah. Zechariah continues,

> "Then the LORD will go out and fight against those nations as when he fights on a day of battle. On that day his feet shall stand on the Mount of Olives that lies before Jerusalem on the east, and the Mount of Olives shall be split in two from east to west by a very wide valley, so that one half of the Mount shall move northward, and the other half southward." (Zech 14:3–4)

The military attack against Jerusalem will trigger the judgement of God upon all these nations. According to Ezekiel, God will actually entice wicked nations to attack Israel in order to then be able to judge them for their wickedness.

> "Thus says the Lord GOD: Behold, I am against you, O Gog, chief prince of Meshech and Tubal. And I will turn you about and put hooks into your jaws, and I will bring you out, and all your army ... You will come up against my people Israel like a cloud covering the land. In the latter days I **will bring you against my land, that the nations may know me, when through you, O Gog, I vindicate my holiness before their eyes.** Thus says the Lord GOD: 'Are you he

of whom I spoke in former days by my servants the prophets of Israel, who in those days prophesied for years that I would bring you against them?'" (Eze 38:3–4,16–17)

Ezekiel continues to prophesy about this army,

"You shall fall on the mountains of Israel, you and all your hordes and the peoples who are with you. I will give you to birds of prey of every sort and to the beasts of the field to be devoured. You shall fall in the open field, for I have spoken, declares the Lord GOD. I will send fire on Magog and on those who dwell securely in the coastlands, and they shall know that I am the LORD. **And my holy name I will make known in the midst of my people Israel, and I will not let my holy name be profaned anymore. And the nations shall know that I am the LORD, the Holy One in Israel.** Behold, it is coming and it will be brought about, declares the Lord GOD. That is the day of which I have spoken." (Eze 39:4–8)

We are called to pray according to these promises. No plans against Jerusalem will succeed!

GOD'S NAME GLORIFIED

God urges us to rejoice over Israel and pray for her salvation, since this will bless the whole world.

"For thus says the LORD: 'Sing aloud with gladness for Jacob, and raise shouts for the chief of the nations: proclaim, give praise, and say, "O LORD, save your people, the remnant of Israel."'" (Jer 31:7)

In contrast to the Land being divided, God's name is glorified when Israel's borders are expanded.

"Therefore say to the house of Israel, Thus says the Lord God: It is not for your sake, O house of Israel, that I am about to act, but for the sake of my holy name, which you have profaned among the nations to which you came. **And I will vindicate the holiness of my great name**, which has been profaned among the nations, and which you have profaned among them. And the nations will know that I am the Lord, declares the Lord God, when through you I vindicate my holiness before their eyes. **I will take you from the nations and gather you from all the countries and bring you into your own land.**" (Eze 36:22–24)

Likewise, Joel prophesied that the Spirit of God will fall upon all flesh when Israel is established:

"**You shall know that I am in the midst of Israel**, and that I am the Lord your God and there is none else. And my people shall never again be put to shame. **And it shall come to pass afterward, that I will pour out my Spirit on all flesh.**" (Joel 2:27–28)

And Paul wrote about Israel, "For if their rejection means the reconciliation of the world, what will their acceptance mean but life from the dead?" (Rom 11:15)

SUMMARY

The church needs to stand on the side of truth according to God's Word and pray for His will to happen. That means to stand firm against a two-state solution and for a one-state solution under the sovereignty of Israel.

1. God will judge all nations that have divided His Land.

2. A two-state solution is the biggest threat to Israel's survival.

3. An Israeli, one-state solution would mean the greatest blessing for both Jews and Arabs. No Arabs in the Middle East have more freedom than the Arabs in Israel.

4. The LORD has promised to bring the counsel of the nations to nothing and frustrate the plans of the peoples (Ps 33:10–11).

5. He has promised to watch over Jerusalem and make the city a heavy stone on which the people will hurt themselves when they try to lift it (Zec 12:3).

6. When God thwarts the people's plans and instead expands Israel's borders, it leads to His Name being glorified all over the earth (Isa 26:15 and Matt 6:9).

CHAPTER 3

WHY ARE THE JEWS SO HATED?

"Behold, a people dwelling alone, and not counting itself among the nations!" —Numbers 23:9

"Then Haman said to King Ahasuerus, 'There is a certain people scattered abroad and dispersed among the peoples in all the provinces of your kingdom. Their laws are different from those of every other people.'" —Esther 3:8

Anti-Semitism means prejudice or hatred against Jews and/or that which is Jewish.[32] It is the oldest and most enduring form of racism in human history. Ever since the days of Pharaoh in Egypt, the Jewish people have always been persecuted.

Each Passover during the traditional seder meal, the Jewish people say, "In every generation they rise up against us to destroy us. But the Holy One, blessed be He, delivers us from their hands."

---

32 A well-known and important definition is the IHRA "working definition of antisemitism" ("What is antisemitism?" IHRA, Dec 20, 2023) *https://holocaustremembrance.com/resources/working-definitions-charters/working-definition-antisemitism*).

Here are some examples from history:

1430 BC	Slavery in Egypt. Pharaoh tries to kill every Jewish boy.
700 BC	Assyria expels the ten tribes from the Northern Kingdom and tries to destroy Jerusalem.
586 BC	Babylon burns Jerusalem and expels the Jews to Babylon.
356 BC	Haman attempts genocide on the Jews.
138 BC	The Greek government prohibits the practice of Judaism in Israel on pain of death.
70 AD	The Romans invade Israel and expel the Jews from Jerusalem.
135 AD	Again the Romans invade Israel and expel the Jews from Jerusalem.
486	Christian monks and mobs burn synagogues, digging up a Jewish cemetery, burning the bones.
624	Mohammed witnesses the beheading of 600 Jews in one day in Medina.
640	Jews expelled from Arabia.
1096	First Crusade: Thousands of Jews are tortured and massacred.
1146	Second Crusade: Thousands of Jews, including women and infants, are slaughtered all across Europe.
13th cent.	The Jews are accused of having caused the Black Death. They are murdered in Frankfurt, Speyer, Koblenz, Mainz, Krakow, Alsace, Bonn, and other cities.
1290	Jews are expelled from England.
1306	Jews are expelled from France.
1349	Jews are expelled from Hungary.
1394	Second expulsion from France.
15th cent.	Jews are accused of murdering Christian children in order to bake unleavened *matzah* bread for Passover with their blood (the "blood libel").
1421	Jews are expelled from Austria.
1492	Jews are expelled from Spain. The Inquisition begins.

1496	Jews are expelled from Portugal.
16th cent.	Jews who secretly preserved their identity are burned in Mexico, Portugal, Peru, and Spain.
1553	The Talmud is burned in Italy.
1648–66	Cossacks, Poles, Russians, and Swedes massacre Jews.
1744	Jews are expelled from Bohemia and Moravia.
1818	Pogroms in Yemen.
1840	Blood libel in Damascus.
1862	General Ulysses S. Grant expels Jews from Tennessee.
1882	Pogroms in Russia.
1917–91	Studying Hebrew constitutes a "criminal offense against the state" in the Soviet Union.
1922 –	Arab Muslim terror against Jews in Israel begins to rise.
1939–45	Six million Jews are murdered across Europe.
1948	Arab countries initiate war to wipe out the State of Israel. Jews flee for their lives from Algeria, Iraq, Syria, Yemen and Egypt.
1964	Palestine Liberation Organization (PLO) is founded with the goal to destroy Israel. It launches terror attacks against Israel from the surrounding Arab nations.
1967	Led by Egypt, neighboring Muslim states commit acts of war against Israel and declare their intention to wipe Israel off the map, leading to the Six Day War.
1973	Egypt and Syria launch a surprise invasion of Israel on the holy day of Yom Kippur in order to destroy Israel.
1979	The Islamic Revolution in Iran proclaims the goal of annihilating Israel.
1982	Iran establishes the Shia terrorist organization Hezbollah in Lebanon with the goal to destroy Israel.
1987	The first Palestinian uprising, Intifada, begins. The Muslim Brotherhood establishes the Palestinian terrorist organization Hamas, with the goal to murder all Jews and destroy Israel.

1993   The Oslo Peace Accords are signed between Israel and PLO, leading instead to suicide bombings and terror.

2000   The Second Intifada begins a wave of terror attacks and suicide bombings all over Israel.

2006   Hezbollah starts the Second Lebanon war against Israel.

2007   Hamas takes control of Gaza, leading to an increase in indiscriminate rockets attacks against civilian targets in Israel and multiple wars with Israel in 2008, 2012, 2014, 2021, and 2023.

2021   U.S. President Biden reestablishes official relations with the Palestinian Authority, violating the Tayler Force Act of 2018, leading to a sharp increase in Palestinian terror attacks in primarily Judea, Samaria, and Jerusalem.

2023   On October 7, Hamas launches a surprise invasion and terror attack into Israel, murdering 1,200 people, mostly civilians, marking the worst atrocity against Jews since the Holocaust. The massacre is supported by 71% of Arabs in Gaza, Judea, and Samaria.[33] Violent, mass protests erupt around the world calling for the murder of Jews and for the end of Israel. Antisemitic attacks skyrocket globally. Russia openly sides with Hamas.

The question that needs to be asked is: what could be the reason for the persistent anti-Semitism and all the constant persecution of the Jewish people throughout history? I will mention five reasons as an explanation.

---

33 "A Palestinian-run survey found that 71% of Palestinians see the decision to attack Israel on October 7th as a good one. 93% do not believe terror organization committed war crimes" (Yitz Goldberg, "Poll: 71% of Palestinian Arabs support October 7th attack," *Israel National News,* March 20, 2024, *https://israelna tionalnews.com/news/387091* [March 20, 2024]).

1. ISRAEL'S ELECTION

The first reason for the long-lasting hatred against the Jewish people is that God chose this people as his own over all other peoples on earth. God says of Israel: "For you are a people holy to the Lord your God. The Lord your God has chosen you to be a people for his treasured possession, out of all the peoples who are on the face of the earth." (Deut 7:6)

King David prayed before the Lord:

> "And who is like your people Israel, the one nation on earth whom God went to redeem to be his people, making himself a name and doing for them great and awesome things by driving out before your people, whom you redeemed for yourself from Egypt, a nation and its gods? And you established for yourself your people Israel to be your people forever. And you, O Lord, became their God." (2 Sam 7:23–24)

Israel is thus a holy people, which God has chosen as his special people, his treasured possession. Note that this election is valid forever. The devil hates everything that belongs to God. In the end, anti-Semitism and hatred of the Jewish people comes from the devil himself. But the election of Israel as God's special people has also aroused strong feelings of jealousy from other peoples throughout history.

However, we need to remember that God's purpose of choosing Israel as his special people, is to bless all the peoples of the earth through them. God said to Abraham when he chose him: "I will make of you a great nation, and I will bless you and make your name great, so that you will be a blessing. I will bless those who bless you, and him who dishonors you I will curse, and in you all the families of the earth shall be blessed." (Gen 12:2–3) He then repeated the same promise to Jacob, "Your offspring shall be like the dust of the earth, and you shall spread abroad to the west and to the east and to the north and to the south, and in you and your offspring shall all the families of the earth be blessed." (Gen 28:14) The election of Israel is included in God's plan of salvation for all mankind. Someone has expressed it in the following way: "For God so loved the world that he chose Israel." Their calling is to bless the whole world.

It is important to remember that this election of the Jewish people for the blessing of the whole world **has not ceased in the New Covenant.** It is not as it is often proclaimed in many Christian traditions, that God chose Israel solely so that Jesus would be born into the world through them, and then their special calling has ended. Peter said to the Jews in the Temple in Jerusalem after Jesus' death and resurrection: **"You are the sons of the prophets and heirs of the covenant that God made with your fathers, saying to Abraham, 'And in your offspring shall all the families of the earth be blessed.'"** (Acts 3:25)

The unique calling and task of the Jewish people to bless the whole world still remains. Paul explains in the letter to the Romans, "Now if their trespass means riches for the world, and if their failure means riches for the Gentiles ... **how much more will their full inclusion** mean! For if their rejection means the reconciliation of the world, **what will their acceptance mean but life from the dead**?" (Rom 11:12, 15) The Jewish people's greatest blessing to the world still lies in the future! We are still waiting to see it—the resurrection from the dead and new life for the whole world.

Christian replacement theology, which entails that the Jews' special status as God's chosen people has ceased and has been transferred to the church, has a very long history that goes all the way back to the first centuries. Unfortunately, it is still deeply rooted in Christian theology today. Replacement theology is a serious identity theft that resulted in an anti-Semitism that has caused endless death and suffering for the Jewish people for the past two thousand years.

2. THE JEWISH PEOPLE ARE DIFFERENT

The second reason for the persistent anti-Semitism is that the Jews are different from all other people on the earth. God says of Israel,

"For you are a people holy to the Lord your God." (Deut 7:6) The word "holy" means "set apart." The Jews are called to be a separate people who are different. Balaam prophesied about Israel, "For from the top of the crags I see him, from the hills I behold him; behold, a people dwelling alone, and not counting itself among the nations!" (Num 23:9)

God made a covenant with Israel on Mount Sinai for them to be His special possession above all other nations on earth. The law was given to them to protect them from the influence of other nations. Paul wrote about this to the Galatians, "Now before faith came, we were held captive under the law, imprisoned until the coming faith would be revealed." (Gal 3:23) This is unfortunately a common negative translation of something that is meant as something positive. There is nothing about any imprisonment in the Greek text. A wall can either be something negative that locks a person in. But a wall can also be something positive that protects a person. The exact same Greek word that is translated as "imprisoned" also appears in Peter's letter, where it says, "who by God's power are being **guarded** through faith for a salvation ready to be revealed in the last time." (1 Pet 1:5) Peter does not mean that through faith we are locked up in a prison, but that through faith we are preserved. In the same way, through the law, the people of Israel have been preserved and protected from perishing. This still applies for Israel and will apply until the day Messiah comes and "all Israel will be saved." (Rom 11:26)

The classic anti-Semite, Haman, who wanted to eradicate the Jewish people in the Persian Empire, said to King Ahasuerus, "There is a certain people scattered abroad and dispersed among the peoples in all the provinces of your kingdom. **Their laws are different from those of every other people**, and they do not keep the king's laws, so that it is not to the king's profit to tolerate them. **If it please the king, let it be decreed that they be destroyed,** and I will pay 10,000 talents of silver into the hands of those who have charge of the king's business, that they may put it into the king's treasuries." (Est 3:8-9) Haman justified his hatred of the Jews by saying that, "Their laws are different from the laws of all other peoples."

The Jewish people's calling to be holy, set apart, and different has not ceased in the New Covenant. All of the New Testament still divides all mankind into those circumcised, i.e. Jews, and the uncircumcised, i.e. Gentiles. Paul wrote about this,

> "Only let each person lead the life that the Lord has assigned to him, and to which God has called him. This is my rule in all the churches. Was anyone at the time of his call already circumcised? Let him not seek to remove the marks of circumcision. Was anyone at the time of his call uncircumcised? Let him not seek circumcision." (1 Cor 7:17-18)

The apostolic rule that Paul established in all congregations was that—while both are saved by grace—Jews and Gentiles have different callings and must remain in their distinct callings, even after coming to faith. If someone was called as circumcised, that is, as a Jew, "let him not seek to remove the marks of circumcision." For this reason the apostles decided, for instance, that Paul and Barnabas should go to the Gentiles with the Gospel, while James, Peter and John would go to the circumcised (Gal 2:9).

The fact that God called the Jewish people to live in obedience to the Law of Moses, makes them a people that is different from all other peoples and this is one of the big reasons why, ever since the law was given on Mount Sinai, they have always been hated and persecuted. The call also includes the conditions God gave them, and the dire consequences that follow when they do not hold fast to the covenant.

3. SALVATION COMES FROM THE JEWS

The third reason for anti-Semitism and the fact that the Jews have always been hated and persecuted, is what Jesus said in his conversation with the Samaritan woman by Jacob's well at Shechem, "You worship what you do not know; we worship what we know, for salvation is from the Jews." (Jn 4:22) Since salvation is from the Jews, the devil has always hated this people and tried to wipe it out.

Everything that has to do with our salvation has come to us from the Jewish people. The Savior of the world was born as a Jew. He was born of a Jewish mother as the newborn king of the Jews (Matt 2:1–2) and was circumcised as a Jew on the eighth day. It was also then that, in accordance with Jewish tradition, he received his name. "And at the end of eight days, when he was circumcised, he was called Jesus, the name given by the angel before he was conceived in the womb." (Lk 2:21)

Jesus then lived his life on earth as a Jewish rabbi in perfect obedience to the law of Moses. When Nathanael understood who Jesus was, he said, "Rabbi, you are the Son of God! You are the King of Israel!" (Jn 1:49) The woman's seed that was going to crush the head of the snake, was both born a Jew and lived as a Jew. This was important to Paul. He wrote to Timothy, "Remember Jesus Christ, risen from the dead, the offspring of David, as preached in my gospel." (2 Tim 2:8) Still today, Jesus identifies himself as a Jew. He says in the last chapter of the Bible, "I, Jesus, have sent my angel to testify to you about these things for the churches. I am the root and the descendant of David, the bright morning star." (Rev 22:16)

The Bible, the Word of God, has also come to us from the Jewish people. "Then what advantage has the Jew? Or what is the value of circumcision? Much in every way. To begin with, the Jews were entrusted with the oracles of God." (Rom 3:1–2) The Gospel has come from Jerusalem through the Jewish apostles. "Thus it is written, that the Messiah should suffer and on the third day rise from the dead, and that repentance for the forgiveness of sins should be proclaimed in his name to all nations, beginning from Jerusalem." (Lk 24:46–47) It is here that the root to our faith is found. Paul addressed the Gentile believers in Rome, "But if some of the branches were broken off, and you, although a wild olive shoot, were grafted in among the others and now share in the nourishing root of the olive tree, do not be arrogant toward the branches. If you are, remember it is not you who support the root, but the root that supports you." (Rom 11:17–18). And further on, "... Macedonia and Achaia have been pleased to make some contribution for the poor among the saints at Jerusalem. For they were pleased to do it, and indeed they owe it to them. For if the Gentiles have come to share in their spiritual blessings, they ought also to be of service to them in material blessings." (Rom 15:26–27) All Gentiles are indebted to the Jewish people for their salvation, because salvation comes from the Jews.

Notice also that Jesus does not simply tell the Samaritan woman that salvation **has come** from the Jews, as if the task of the Jews in God's plan of salvation for the world was completed in connection with the first coming of Jesus. He says that salvation **comes** from the Jews in the present tense as something continuous. The Jewish people also have the key to the return of Jesus. It is when they as a people, primarily through their leadership, welcome him to Jerusalem, that he will return.

> "O Jerusalem, Jerusalem, the city that kills the prophets and stones those who are sent to it! How often would I have gathered your children together as a hen gathers her brood under her wings, and you were not willing! See, your house is left to you desolate. For I tell you, you will not see me again, until you say, 'Blessed is he who comes in the name of the Lord.'" (Matt 23:37–39)

This means that the Jews must be gathered back to Jerusalem before Jesus can return. They must be in place in Jerusalem, and specifically on the Temple Mount, before this promise can be fulfilled. Jesus cites Psalm 118 from where it says, "Blessed is he who comes in the name of the Lord! We bless you from the house of the Lord." (Ps 118:26). It was also exactly in that place that Jesus quoted the first part of the verse when he said, "For I tell you, [you Jewish leaders here on the Temple Mount] you will not see me again, until you say, 'Blessed is he who comes in the name of the Lord.'" (Matt 23:39) "Blessed is he who comes" is the Hebrew way of saying "welcome."

It is because salvation comes from the Jews that the devil hates the Jewish people so intensely and has always wanted to destroy them. "In every generation they rise up against us to destroy us. But the Holy One, blessed be He, delivers us from their hands."

4. THE JEWS HAVE THE COVENANTS AND THE PROMISES

Paul explains about the Jewish people, "They are Israelites, and to them belong ... the covenants ... and the promises." (Rom 9:4) Because the Jewish people have both the "covenants ... and the promises," the devil has concentrated his efforts on trying to wipe out the Jewish people in order to nullify God's promises. This is the fourth reason for the persistant anti-Semitism and the persecution of the Jewish people.

Hitler, who wanted to establish a thousand-year, Aryan world empire, was neither the first nor the last one that has tried to destroy the Jewish people. All kingdoms in history that have sought global dominion have had the same aspiration, Egypt, Assyria, Babylonia, Persia, Greece, Rome, and unfortunately, also the Christian church's replacement theology. No one has actually been as cruel in their persecution of the Jewish people as the replacement theological church has been, and this does not only apply to the Catholic, but also the Protestant church. Hitler could say that he did nothing to the

Jews other than what Luther advocated in his infamous book, *The Jews and Their Lies*.[34]

Islamists have the same objective as Hitler had, to create a global empire, and therefore, they share the same aspiration to wipe out the Jewish people. The same is true of communism. The devil knows that God has made an everlasting covenant with Israel and promised them to bless the whole world with a thousand-year kingdom of justice and peace from Jerusalem.

> "The word that Isaiah the son of Amoz saw concerning Judah and Jerusalem. It shall come to pass in the latter days that the mountain of the house of the LORD shall be established as the highest of the mountains, and shall be lifted up above the hills; and all the nations shall flow to it, and many peoples shall come, and say: 'Come, let us go up to the mountain of the LORD, to the house of the God of Jacob, that he may teach us his ways and that we may walk in his paths.' For out of Zion shall go forth the law, and the word of the LORD from Jerusalem. He shall judge between the nations, and shall decide disputes for many peoples; and they shall beat their swords into plowshares, and their spears into pruning hooks; nation shall not lift up sword against nation, neither shall they learn war anymore. O house of Jacob, come, let us walk in the light of the LORD." (Is 2:1-5)

The disciples' last question to Jesus was, "Lord, will you at this time restore the kingdom to Israel?" (Acts 1:6) Jesus did not rebuke

---

34 Cf. Michael L. Brown, *Michael L. Brown, Our Hands Are Stained With Blood: The Tragic Story of the "Church" and the Jewish People (Shippensburg, PA: Destiny Image Publishers, 1992).* Brown cites Dennis Prager and Joseph Telushkin, who wrote, "Christianity did not create the Holocaust; indeed Nazism was anti-Christian, but it made it possible. Without Christian antisemitism, the Holocaust would have been inconceivable." (p. 7)

them for the question but answered, "It is not for you to know times or seasons that the Father has fixed by his own authority." (Acts 1:7) First, the Gospel must be preached throughout the whole world as a testimony to all peoples. Then the end will come, when Jesus, as Israel's King and Messiah, sits on the throne of his father David in Jerusalem to rule over the whole earth and restore the kingdom to Israel.

The devil hates the fulfillment of God's promises because then his time to steal, kill, and destroy will be over. He will first be bound for a thousand years and then, after a short time, be thrown forever in the burning lake of fire. Since the promises belong to Israel, the devil has therefore tried to wipe out the Jewish people. If he succeeds in this, God will no longer be able to fulfill his promises, and then the devil has won. He has constantly been striving for this, ever since God chose Israel. This is yet another reason for the persistent anti-Semitism.

5. THE CALLING INCLUDES SPECIAL GIFTS

With a divine calling, gifts and blessings that are necessary to fulfill the calling, also follow. Paul writes about these gifts, "As regards the gospel, they are enemies for your sake. But as regards election, they are beloved for the sake of their forefathers. **For the gifts and the calling of God are irrevocable**." (Rom 11:28–29) This is the fifth reason why the Jewish people have always been persecuted—pure jealousy because of the gifts God has given them.

Today, Israel is a small country with just under 10 million inhabitants in an area, just slightly larger than the state of New Jersey. Nevertheless, Israel is today counted as one of the world's ten most powerful nations. This is supernatural. It is because of the unique gifts that God has given to the Jewish people. 22% of all Nobel prizes over the years have gone to Jews, despite the fact that they make up no more than 0.002% of the world's population. This means that Jewish Nobel laureates are overrepresented by 11,250% compared to other ethnic groups. This is not only due to a higher average IQ among Jews, but above all to strong Jewish traditions of prioritizing education, including hard work and perseverance. Israel's most famous rabbi from the Middle Ages, Maimonides, declared that it is forbidden to interrupt, or disturb young people studying, even at the cost of rebuilding the Temple.

The Jewish mentality also includes not being satisfied with the status quo, but always looking for new solutions. The Jews have always been different. When Jacob set out for Haran to look for a wife, it says:

> "Then Jacob went on his journey and came to the land of the people of the east. As he looked, he saw a well in the field, and behold, three flocks of sheep lying beside it, for out of that well the flocks were watered. The stone on the well's mouth was large, and when all the flocks were gathered there, the shepherds would roll the stone from the mouth of the well and water the sheep, and put the stone back in its place over the mouth of the well. Jacob said to them, ... 'Behold, it is still high day; it is not time for the livestock to be gathered together. Water the sheep and go, pasture them.' But they said, 'We cannot until all the flocks are gathered together and the stone is rolled from the mouth of the well; then we water the sheep.' ... Now as soon as Jacob saw Rachel the daughter of Laban his mother's brother, and the sheep of Laban his mother's brother, Jacob came near and rolled the stone from the well's mouth and watered the flock of Laban his mother's brother." (Gen 29:1–10)

Jacob did not accept the explanation he received that one had to wait until all the flocks were in place, before giving the sheep water to drink. He broke with established customs and came up with a way to be able to give water to the sheep at once. Israel has become known as the "start-up nation" because of all the new inventions that are being made in the country today, which leads to new profitable companies constantly being started.

When Jacob had been with his uncle Laban in Haran for 20 years, he had become very wealthy, even though Laban kept deceiving him. It says: "Now Jacob heard that the sons of Laban were saying, 'Jacob has taken all that was our father's, and from what was our father's he has gained all this wealth.' And Jacob saw that Laban did not regard him with favor as before. Then the Lord said to Jacob, 'Return to the land of your fathers and to your kindred, and I will be with you.'" (Gen 31:1–3) Jacob had not taken anything from Laban, but God had blessed him. He explained to his father-in-law how it happened,

> "These twenty years I have been in your house. I served you fourteen years for your two daughters, and six years for your flock, and you have changed my wages ten times. If the God of my father, the God of Abraham and the Fear of Isaac, had not been on my side, surely now you would have sent me away empty-handed. God saw my affliction and the labor of my hands and rebuked you last night." (Gen 31:41–42)

In the same way, God has blessed many Jews during their two thousand year long dispersion, and given some of them great wealth. When throughout history Jews were forbidden to participate in the labor market and to be part of society, they had to go their own way and seek the few occupations that remained. For example, they became pioneers with new methods of banking still in use today. Some found success in the diamond trade. Later, the Jews were accused by the same communities that forbade them to enter other professions. Just like for Jakob, it had led to jealousy and hostility from those around. This is also an explanation for the widespread anti-Semitism today.

A PRIESTLY NATION

God has called the Jewish people to be a priestly people. It is written about the restoration of Israel:

> "They shall build up the ancient ruins; they shall raise up the former devastations; they shall repair the ruined cities, the devastations of many generations. Strangers shall stand and tend your flocks; foreigners shall be your plowmen and vinedressers; but you shall be called the priests of the LORD; they shall speak of you as the ministers of our God; you shall eat the wealth of the nations, and in their glory you shall boast." (Is 61:4–6)

A priestly service includes teaching. God has undoubtedly given Jews a tremendous gift to be able to communicate. A classic anti-Semitic lie is that the Jews control Hollywood and all media in the world. This is certainly not true, but the accusation is based on the fact that many Jews are very prominent in media, communication, writing, and teaching. It is another gifting that God has given them.

God has undeniably blessed the Jewish people in a unique way, just as he promised Abraham, "And I will make of you a great nation, and I will bless you and make your name great, so that you will be a blessing... in you all the families of the earth shall be blessed." (Gen 12:2–3) Peter repeated this promise to the Jews in Jerusalem, "You are the sons of the prophets and of the covenant that God made with your fathers, saying to Abraham, 'And in your offspring shall all the families of the earth be blessed.'" (Acts 3:25) Jews have a unique ability to excel everywhere they go. When the gifts God has given them are used properly, it leads to great blessing. When Jewish people get into the wrong context and the gifts are misused, it unfortunately leads to an equally strong curse. In both cases, it often results in jealousy and hostility, just as we read about Jacob.

THE CALLING ENTAILS DISCIPLINE

The unique calling God has given the Jewish people to be a nation of priests for the whole world, also means that they are under special discipline. Amos prophesies about this:

> "Hear this word that the Lord has spoken against you, O people of Israel, against the whole family that I brought up out of the land of Egypt: 'You only have I known of all the families of the earth; therefore I will punish you for all your iniquities.' Do two walk together, unless they have agreed to meet?" (Amos 3:1–3)

God calls Israel his "firstborn son." The Book of Hebrews cites the Proverb, "My son, do not despise the Lord's discipline or be weary of his reproof, for the Lord reproves him whom he loves, as a father the son in whom he delights." (Prov 3:11–12) Israel, especially during the last two thousand years of dispersion, has had to go through a furnace of suffering more than other nations. In the film *Fiddler on the Roof,* the simple Jew, Tevye, contemplates his personal trials in light of the Jews being God's chosen people. He finally expresses his despair to God, "Once in a while, can't you choose someone else?"

In Romans, Paul likens Israel to a cultivated olive tree, compared to all other nations, who are likened to wild olive trees. "For if you were cut from what is by nature a wild olive tree, and grafted, contrary to nature, into a cultivated olive tree, how much more will these, the natural branches, be grafted back into their own olive tree." (Rom 11:24)

A cultivated olive tree receives fertilizer and extra nutrition, but it is also pruned to bear more fruit. The Jewish people have "the adoption, the glory, the covenants, the giving of the law, the worship, and the promises." (Rom 9:4) But they have also had to go through more suffering and persecution than any other people—all in order to be the instrument that God will use to bless the whole world with "life from the dead" (Rom 11:15) when the kingdom is restored to Israel (Acts 1:6).

After the promise in Isaiah that the Jewish people will be called the priests of the Lord, it says,

> "Instead of your shame there shall be a double portion; instead of dishonor they shall rejoice in their lot; therefore in their land they shall possess a double portion; they shall have everlasting joy. For I the Lord love justice; I hate robbery and wrong; I will faithfully give them their recompense, and I will make an everlasting covenant with them. Their offspring shall be known among the nations, and their descendants in the midst of the peoples; all who see them shall acknowledge them, that they are an offspring the Lord has blessed." (Is 61:7–9)

God cannot exalt those who have never first been tried in the furnace of suffering. We read of the sufferings and hardships that King David had to go through before God could place him on the throne over Israel. Likewise, it is written about Jesus, "For it was fitting that he, for whom and by whom all things exist, in bringing many sons to glory, should make the founder of their salvation perfect through suffering ... Although he was a son, he learned obedience through what he suffered. And being made perfect, he became the source of eternal salvation to all who obey him." (Heb 2:10; 5:8–9) All the psalms that David wrote about his hardships and sufferings are not merely messianic prophecies, but have an application to Israel.

Anti-Semitism, the suffering and persecution that the Jewish people have had to endure during its two-thousand-year-long *Via Dolorosa*, is in itself proof that they are God's chosen people. Election, suffering, and exaltation go together.

There is nothing new under the sun. During Passover, Jews have for centuries been accused of baking and eating unleavened *matzah* bread made from the blood of Christian children—despite the fact that all Jews are strictly forbidden from consuming blood. In the Middle Ages, they were accused of the Black Death. Therefore, it is no surprise that the Jewish State is now accused of genocide in Gaza, as Israel tries to defend its population against an inhumanly cruel terrorist organization that uses civilians as human shields, while Israel does everything possible—far beyond any other country's military—to avoid civilian casualties. Anti-Zionism is today's form of the eternal anti-Semitism.

CHAPTER 4

TWO WIDESPREAD LIES ABOUT THE JEWS

"[The devil] was a murderer from the beginning, and does not stand in the truth, because there is no truth in him. When he lies, he speaks out of his own character, for he is a liar and the father of lies." (John 8:44)

THE PROTOCOLS OF THE ELDERS OF ZION

A "false flag operation" is a secret, covert action carried out with the aim of deceiving the public into believing that what has happened has been done by people other than those that in reality performed the action. The purpose is to give another the blame for what you yourself have done.

Probably the most successful example of a false flag operation—at least in modern history—is a forged document that goes by many different names, but is usually called *The Protocols of the Elders of Zion,* or "The Protocols." This fictional hate screed against the Jewish people was first published in its entirety in 1905 in a book titled *The*

Large in the Small, written by a Russian religious fanatic and occultist named Sergei Nilus. From there, it has since spread all over the world and has been translated into every major language on earth. Before Nilus included it in his book, only parts of the false document had been spread in various newspapers and leaflets in Tsarist Russia, but never in its entirety.

The contents are allegedly notes from secret meetings with a global, Jewish power elite who seek to break down Christianity's influence and, step by step, take power over the whole world. The document was originally produced by the Russian secret police, the Okhrana, with the aim of blaming the Jews for the disintegration of Tsarist Russia and inciting pogroms against them. In Russia, however, the writing had a limited effect, due to the fact that the Jews in Russia at that time were very poor. The common people found it difficult to believe that Jews could be behind a plan to conquer the world. In addition, the Russians were used to the secret police's methods of producing forgeries, with the result that not many people believed *The Protocols.*

However, the document spread rapidly in other parts of the world. It became like a flaming torch in a powder keg in anti-Semitic circles, especially in Europe. In Germany, it led rather quickly to the murder of the Jewish foreign minister of the Weimar Republic, Walter Rathenau, in 1922. The murderers committed suicide, but their driver, Ernst Techow, defended himself in the subsequent trial by referencing the contents of *The Protocols* and claiming that he had done a good deed in helping to kill Rathenau the Jew.

Another German who got ahold of the writing was a young man from Austria, named Adolf Hitler. He referred to the document in his book *Mein Kampf. The Protocols* came to form the foundation of Hitler's and the Nazis' hatred of Jews and the main motivation behind the extermination of over six million Jews in Europe. Hitler made sure, among other things, to spread this hateful book to all school children in Germany for free.

The Protocols also quickly fell into the hands of Muslim Islamists in the Middle East, just as the major Jewish waves of return to Palestine began. Both *Mein Kampf* and *The Protocols of the Elders of Zion* have been bestsellers in the Arab world for almost a hundred years. Hamas refers to *The Protocols* in its Charter. This poisoned screed from the Abyss—along with the old Muslim *hadith* to kill all Jews hiding behind rocks and trees—is the primary motivation for Hamas' manifesto to wipe out Israel and exterminate all Jews worldwide. Like Ernst Techow, who participated in murdering Rathenau the Jew, Hamas and millions of Muslims today around the world see the annihilation of all Jews as a benefit to mankind, based on *The Protocols of the Elders of Zion*. Just as it is expressed in the introduction to Hamas' Charter: "Our struggle against the Jews is very great and very serious. It needs all sincere efforts."

Another person who drew attention to *The Protocols* and spread the forgery as much as possible around the world under the title *The International Jew,* was industrial magnate Henry Ford. Because of this, he was eventually put on trial in the United States for defamation. However, before any verdict could be made in the case, a settlement was reached between the parties, in which Henry Ford promised to withdraw all rights to translate and distribute the forgery in other countries, to destroy all copies that were still in his possession, and to pay damages of an unknown amount to the Jews who took him to trial. However, this did not prevent the book from continuing to spread, both in the U.S. and beyond. Quite the opposite! Those who translated the writing and printed it did not care that Henry Ford had pulled the rights for it, and Ford himself made no effort to prevent them. It is worth noting that Henry Ford's hometown, Dearborn, Michigan, has for many years been the Muslim Brotherhood's main stronghold in their quest to gain power and influence in the United States.

LACKING LOGIC

Henry Ford, as well as essentially everyone—including Hamas—who believe in the contents of *The Protocols* (that there really is a global Jewish elite working to take over the world, despite evidence to the contrary) defend themselves by saying, "It is enough to look at world developments to see that it is exactly according to what is written in *The Protocols of the Elders of Zion*. No further evidence is needed. Reality confirms that the content is true."

It is for this reason that I call *The Protocols* the most successful false flag operation in history. The fact that the content matches the developments we see in the world, does not automatically prove that it is the Jewish people who are behind it. In recent years, it has become apparent to an increasing number of people that there really is a financial elite striving for global dominion. The World Economic Forum, for example, is quite open about it. Today, the world's resources are increasingly concentrated in the hands of a few, super-rich billionaires, several of them managing more resources than entire countries. The way they operate bears great resemblance to the writings in *The Protocols*.

It is also true that some of these super-billionaires are Jews. But that is where the similarities end. Not all of these billionaires are Jews. And their agenda definitely has nothing to do with either Zion, Zionism, or Judaism! The billionaires behind the World Economic Forum are neither Zionists nor religious Jews, although some of them are ethnic Jews. But far from all of them are Jews. This fact alone shows that *The Protocols* is a false flag operation, since in spite of the facts, the Jewish people are being blamed for something of which they are innocent. This is just like what Hitler did, and just like Hamas and many others are doing today.

That this false flag operation still succeeded to such an extent in duping so many, despite the facts which should be obvious to everyone, has exactly the same explanation as the reasons for the long-lived anti-Semitism in the world. The Jewish people are different from all other peoples. Since they are also fewer than almost all other peoples, it has been easy to make Jews into scapegoats. The fact that Jews have been successful in most areas where they have involved themselves, has only added jealousy to the hatred. Therefore, throughout history, they have been blamed for basically all the misery in the world, from the Black Death to all wars.

On top of all this, the Jewish people have a calling from God to bless the whole world from Jerusalem when the Messiah comes and the kingdom is restored to Israel. Satan hates this calling. Therefore, through *The Protocols,* with all his cunning and shrewdness, he has done his utmost to produce a lying, distorted version of the calling of the Jewish people, to arouse the envy and wrath of the world against them, in an attempt to abort God's plan.

THE PROTOCOLS EXPOSED

The origins of *The Protocols of the Elders of Zion* were revealed at a trial in Bern, Switzerland in 1935. The Swiss Federation of Jewish Communities put the Swiss Nazi Party on trial regarding the distribution of *The Protocols,* accusing them of spreading "obscene literature," which was banned in Switzerland at that time.[35]

The trial involved the following questions:

1. Was *The Protocols of the Elders of Zion* a forgery?

2. Was it plagiarized?

3. If it was, what was its source?

4. Can *The Protocols* be classified as obscene literature?

---

35 Cf. Hadassa Ben-Itto, *The Lie that Wouldn't Die* (Portland, OR: Vallentine-Mitchell, 2005).

Attorney Georges Brunschvig, who was the prosecutor for the Jewish federation during the trial, could produce evidence that the document was originally written in French during the years 1896–1900 by a man named Matvei Golovinskii, who was commissioned by Piotr Rachkowskii, the Russian Okhrana's chief agent in Paris. The document was then translated into Russian in St. Petersburg, from where it was later spread all over the world.

Two Russian noblewomen in Paris, Katerina Radzivill and Henriette Hurblut, independently testified at the trial that Golovinskii had shown them the handwritten original in Paris and had told them about the purpose of the document. A man named Armand Alexander du Chayla also later saw the original in Russia. All three confirmed the appearance of the handwritten document, which had, among other things, a large blue stain from an ink pen on the front.

The Tsarist secret police in Paris had used two sources for writing *The Protocols*:

Source A: The first was an extract from a novel, an anti-Semitic pamphlet entitled: *In the Jewish Cemetery in Prague*. The pamphlet was originally a chapter with the same name in a historical political novel called *Biarritz*. It was published in 1868 by the German Herman Goedsche under the pseudonym Sir John Ratcliffe. Goedsche had been fired from his job within the German state after he, with the help of a forged document, had tried to slander the German democratic leadership. Goedsche then tried his hand at becoming an author.

In the Jewish Cemetery in Prague tells a story of how representatives from the twelve tribes of Israel gather once every century around the grave of a rabbi in Prague to plan the victory of Judaism over Christianity and the whole world. At these gatherings, they also report on successes they have made during the past century. They all swear an oath to a golden calf surrounded by fire that rises from the rabbi's grave. Satan himself then speaks to them from the grave.

The pamphlet was spread in Russia to incite pogroms against the Jews. In France, the pamphlet was published under the title *The Rab-*

bi's Speech. Now, Goedsche, a.k.a. Ratcliffe, claimed that his fantasy was based on fact. It was this anti-Semitic pamphlet that gave the chief of the Russian secret police in Paris, Rachkowskii, the idea of writing a more substantial publication against the Jews, which he decided to call *The Protocols of the Elders of Zion.*

Source B: The second source for *The Protocols* was a 1860s French book, *Dialogue in Hell,* written by a Freemason in Paris named Maurice Joly. Almost two-thirds of *The Protocols* are direct quotations from Joly's book. *Dialogue in Hell* describes a conversation in hell between Montesquieu and Machiavelli about the best way for a minority to take control of a society through terror, lies, and bribery. The book had been banned and confiscated in France at a trial against Joly in 1865. However, one copy was kept at the National Library in Paris, where it was copied by hand by Rachkowskii's assistant Golovinskii. Certain sections of Joly's book had been marked in pencil. They turned out to be identical to the sections that were copied and used in *The Protocols.* Philip Graves, *The Times* correspondent in Istanbul, was the first person to expose this plagiarism already in 1921. A copy had been discovered, published in Geneva in 1864. Maurice Joly's *Dialogue in Hell* had 25 chapters. *The Protocols* has 24 chapters. **It is critically important to note that Joly's book had nothing to do with Jews.** But *Dialogue in Hell* was largely copied by Rachkowskii and Golovinskii to use against the Jews.

It is no coincidence that *The Protocols* was fabricated in Paris, as France at that time was characterized by extremely widespread anti-Semitism, of which the infamous Dreyfus Affair was one example. Alfred Dreyfus was a Jewish officer in the French army who was falsely accused of treason and sentenced in 1894 to life imprisonment on Devil's Island. He was released after five years and then fully exonerated in 1906.

***The Protocols of the Elders of Zion* arose from a combination of French ideas and Russian tactics, in an environment marked by deep-rooted anti-Semitism, intrigues, forgeries, occultism, and freemasonry.**

The Christian judge at the trial in Bern, Walter Meyer, ruled in his final judgment that *The Protocols of the Elders of Zion* was beyond all doubts a forgery and largely a plagiarism of Maurice Joly's book. However, he acquitted the representatives of the Swiss Nazi Party because he did not find it possible to classify the contents of the document as "obscene literature."

It is quite clear that *The Protocols of the Elders of Zion* is a forgery. It is not only a forgery, but the majority was plagiarized from a French book that had nothing to do with the Jewish people. Despite the verdict in the Bern trial, this forgery has continued to spread throughout the world with a devastating and deadly outcome for millions of Jews, above all, through the Holocaust and Islamist terror against Jews around the world today. Those who defend the document, refer—just like Henry Ford—to the fact that it is enough to study world developments for the past century. Once this connects with an already preconceived, anti-Semitic attitude, the matter is settled.

That world developments are similar to the plan for world domination presented in *The Protocols*, indicates that there are other actors (including spiritual principalities and powers) who have successfully applied these principles, but managed to blame the Jews for it. *The Protocols of the Elders of Zion* thus constitutes the most successful and devastating false flag operation in history, which has cost the lives of millions of innocent Jews. This blatant forgery is a cunningly calculated, diabolical lie from hell that won't die. There are surprisingly many—even among highly educated and intellectual people who consider themselves critical thinkers—who today firmly believe this lie about the Jewish people.

"KHAZAR JEWS"

Another long-standing lie about the Jewish people that has become increasingly popular in recent decades, is the claim that the Ashkenazi Jews of Europe and America are not real Jews. Rather, they originate from the Khazars, a Turkish people group that for the last millennium populated the Caucasus region north of the Black and Caspian Seas. According to this theory, the Khazars converted to Judaism in the ninth century and today constitute the Ashkenazi Jews.

This false theory is becoming ever more popular among anti-Semites and anti-Zionists in order to deprive the Ashkenazi Jews of their connection to the Land of Israel.

According to the theory, the Ashkenazi Jews of Europe have no right to claim Israel as their original homeland. They are not real Jews, but constitute a foreign people group with a false identity, without any right to settle in Israel. The "Palestinians" have a far greater connection and right to the Land of Israel. On this basis, some even claim that Hitler murdered the "wrong people." He did not really exterminate any Jews in Europe, only "Khazars."

However, there are several facts, both biblical and scientific, that refute this myth about the Ashkenazi Jews.

First, those who hold to the Khazar theory as an argument against Israel, often ignore the fact that more than half of today's Jews in Israel are not Ashkenazi Jews. The majority are Mizrahi, i.e. dark-skinned, Middle Eastern Jews who were forced to escape Muslim countries after 1948. This obvious truth is often lacking in anti-Zionist theories.

Secondly, it is very clear from the Bible that God promised to preserve the Jewish people as his special people. "Hear the word of the Lord, O nations, and declare it in the coastlands far away; say, 'He who scattered Israel will gather him, and will keep him as a shepherd keeps his flock.'" (Jer 31:10)

The Jewish people have not dissolved, disappeared, or been replaced by another people. God has promised to preserve the Jewish people in the same way as a shepherd watches over his flock. Here is another biblical promise about this,

> "Thus says the Lord, who gives the sun for light by day and the fixed order of the moon and the stars for light by night, who stirs up the sea so that its waves roar—

the Lord of hosts is his name: 'If this fixed order departs from before me, declares the Lord, then shall the offspring of Israel cease from being a nation before me forever.' Thus says the Lord: 'If the heavens above can be measured, and the foundations of the earth below can be explored, then I will cast off all the offspring of Israel for all that they have done, declares the Lord.'" (Jer 31:35–37)

There are those who believe that there is historical evidence that the leading dynasty among the Khazars converted to Judaism in the ninth century. This is not impossible, although the majority of the Khazars actually converted to Islam. Such conversions to Judaism have taken place throughout history. In the book of Esther, for example, it says that many people converted to Judaism. "And many from the peoples of the country declared themselves Jews, for fear of the Jews had fallen on them." (Est 8:17) Even today, the Moabite Ruth—who is part of Jesus' genealogy and who said to Naomi, "Your people are my people and your God is my God"—represents the role model for conversion of Gentiles to become Jews.

That all Ashkenazi Jews today are descendents from the Khazars is a myth that is not supported by serious scientific research. Dr. Alexander Beider is one of the many who have clarified this,

"The theory received a recent boost with the 1976 publication of 'The Thirteenth Tribe,' a book by Arthur Koestler. Most recently, the Khazarian hypothesis has been promoted by authors like the Tel Aviv University professor of history Shlomo Sand and Tel Aviv University professor of linguistics Paul Wexler, as well the geneticist Eran Elhaik. Despite this institutional backing, the theory is absolutely without evidence. ... [N]o direct historiographical data is available to connect the Jews who lived in Eastern Europe in the 14th century with their co-religionists from the 10th-century Khazaria."[36]

Dr. Beider clarifies, "In addition to history and linguistics, a third discipline can help us put to rest the Khazarian hypothesis: onomastics, or the study of proper names." He states categorically, "The corpus of personal names and surnames borne by Jews in Eastern Europe during the last six centuries, as well as the Yiddish language as a whole, do not contain any link to Khazaria."[37]

Biblical scholar and theologian Dr. Michael Brown has put it this way,

> "Ashkenazi Jews can ultimately trace back to a smaller number of families that directly trace back to the children of Israel. They were in exile, and then, in reaching certain parts of Europe, began to intermarry. Others married in with them. In other words, the joining of others to the Jewish people, as has happened with Ruth and others, like Rahab, throughout history. They married in, and that's why we have this diversity, that's why you have Jews with all different color skin ... But ultimately, this [Ashkenazi heritage] can be traced through DNA, this can be traced linguistically, this can be traced historically, this can be traced archaeologically, this can be traced in every way you can trace. We

---

36 Alexander Beider, "Ashkenazi Jews Are Not Khazars. Here's The Proof," *Forward* (Sep 25, 2017), *https://forward.com/opinion/382967/ashkenazi-jews-are-not-khazars-heres-the-proof* [Dec 22, 2023]. Cf. Prof. Shaul Stampfer, "New study finds no evidence that Ashkenazi Jews are the descendants of Khazars, or that subjects in the medieval kingdom converted to Judaism en masse." ("Jews Are Not Descended From Khazars, Hebrew University Historian Says," *Haaretz*, June 26, 2014, *https://www.haaretz.com/jewish/2014-06-26/ty-article/khazar-myth-busted/0000017f-db86-df62-a9ff-dfd788d80000* [Dec 22, 2023]).

37 Ibid.

can say as Ashkenazi Jews that our ultimate roots go back to Abraham, Isaac, and Jacob—the children of Israel in the land [of Israel]."[38]

We can thus, on historical, genetic, linguistic, and onomastic grounds, reject the myth of so-called "Khazar Jews" that anti-Semites and anti-Zionists like to posit in order to slander Jews. One of many who today uses this slur is the openly anti-Semitic, Palestinian-American congresswoman Rashida Tlaib.

Another typical example is David Anderson, one of the perpetrators behind the murders of three people in a Jewish kosher shop in the Greenville neighborhood of Jersey City in 2019. In 2015, he wrote on Facebook: "Brooklyn is full of Nazis—Ashke-Nazis (Khazars)."

Lies about Jews always begin with words, but often end, as in this case, with murder and bloodshed.

---

38 Michael L. Brown, "Debunking the Khazar Myth," *ASKDrBrown* (May 2, 2020), *https://www.youtube.com/watch?v=kdNoBaoT5Yo* [Dec 22, 2023].

CHAPTER 5

THE BATTLE FOR THE TRUTH

*"Then I saw heaven opened, and behold, a white horse! The one sitting on it is called **Faithful and True**, and in righteousness he judges and makes war ... He is clothed in a robe dipped in blood, and the name by which he is called is The Word of God." —Revelation 19:11, 13*

In the end times, Satan will do everything in his power to slander and accuse Israel in an attempt to then wipe out God's people. His goal is to turn the whole world against Israel because they are the people who have received the promises of salvation for the whole world. The final battle over Israel and Jerusalem, that will culminate in the battle at Armageddon, is first and foremost a spiritual battle for the truth. The enemy, who will try to wipe out Israel, is called "the father of lies" (Jn 8:44) He is "the great dragon ... that ancient serpent, who is called the devil and Satan, the deceiver of the whole world." (Rev 12:9) Satan literally means "accuser" or "adversary." The word devil literally means "slanderer." Satan is looking to accuse and slander Israel. He is also called "a murderer from the beginning" (John 8:44), because murder and death have always been the end goal of his lies, from the very start.

Antichrist, who physically will lead the battle against Israel, is called "the liar" by John (1 Jn 2:22). Daniel prophesies about him, "and it will throw truth to the ground, and it will act and prosper." (Dan 8:12) Antichrist's opponent is the Messiah, who is "the Truth." (Jn 14:6) The sword that proceeds from the mouth of Messiah when he returns to judge the whole world, is the Word of God, which is the truth.

> "Then I saw heaven opened, and behold, a white horse! The one sitting on it is called Faithful and True, and in righteousness he judges and makes war. His eyes are like a flame of fire, and on his head are many diadems, and he has a name written that no one knows but himself. He is clothed in a robe dipped in blood, and the name by which he is called is The Word of God. And the armies of heaven, arrayed in fine linen, white and pure, were following him on white horses. From his mouth comes a sharp sword with which to strike down the nations, and he will rule them with a rod of iron. He will tread the winepress of the fury of the wrath of God the Almighty. On his robe and on his thigh he has a name written, King of kings and Lord of lords." (Rev 19:11–16)

Jesus prayed to the Father for all his disciples, "Sanctify them in the truth, your word is truth." (Jn 17:17) The battle between the Messiah and the antichrist, between the truth and the liar, is also described in Psalm 45,

> "In your majesty ride out victoriously for the cause of truth and meekness and righteousness; let your right hand teach you awesome deeds! Your arrows are sharp in the heart of the king's enemies; the peoples fall under you." (Ps 45:4–5)

So, the enemy that we are fighting is:

1. The Father of Lies (John 8:44a)
2. Deceiver (Rev 12:9)
3. Accuser and slanderer (Rev 12:10)
4. Adversary (1 Pet 5:8)
5. Murderer (John 8:44)
6. Antichrist, who is called the Liar (1 Jn 2:22)

We can read more about the final battle against Israel in the book of Revelation. Chapter 17 says,

> "The ten horns you saw are ten kings who have not yet received a kingdom, but who for one hour will receive authority as kings along with the beast. They have one purpose and will give their power and authority to the beast. They will wage war against the Lamb, but the **Lamb will triumph over them** because he is Lord of lords and King of kings— **and with him will be his called, chosen and faithful followers.**" (Rev. 17:12–14 NIV)

Here we see that those who are **called, chosen and faithful** are also involved together with the Messiah in the final battle for the truth against the lie. It says in chapter 19 that "The heavenly hosts followed him on white horses, and they were clothed in white, clean linen." Those who were victorious over the beast, the antichrist, will be with Messiah when he comes to destroy him! "And then the lawless one will be revealed, whom the Lord will consume with the breath of His mouth and destroy with the brightness of His coming." (2 Thess 2:8) Hallelujah!

THE BATTLE FOR THE LAND OF ISRAEL

The Bible is very clear about Judea and Samaria, the area that the world media calls the West Bank and that the "Palestinians" demand for their state. In Ezekiel 36, the area is called the "Mountains of Israel." God himself says of this area that it is "My land."

> "Therefore thus says the Lord GOD: Surely I have spoken in my hot jealousy against the rest of the nations and against all Edom, who gave my land to themselves as a possession with wholehearted joy and utter contempt, that they might make its pasturelands a prey. Therefore prophesy concerning the land of Israel, and say to the mountains and hills, to the ravines and valleys, Thus says the Lord GOD: Behold, I have spoken in my jealous wrath, because you have suffered the reproach of the nations. Therefore thus says the Lord GOD: I swear that the nations that are all around you shall themselves suffer reproach. But you, O mountains of Israel, shall shoot forth your branches and yield your fruit to my people Israel, for they will soon come home. " (Eze 36:5–8)

The "battle on the great day of God the Almighty," will be the battle to destroy Israel. In Revelation 16:15 it says, "Behold, I am coming like a thief! Blessed is the one who stays awake keeping his garments on, that he may not go about naked and be seen exposed!" We must be awake and aware of what is happening today, so we are not surprised but are ready for the return of Jesus.

> "And I saw, coming out of the mouth of the dragon and out of the mouth of the beast and out of the mouth of the false prophet, three unclean spirits like frogs. **For they are demonic spirits, performing signs, who go abroad to the kings of the whole world, to assemble them for battle on the great day of God the Almighty**." (Rev 16:13-14)

The three evil spirits who are likened to frogs and who deceive the leaders of the earth to turn against Israel are:

1. **Anti-Semitism**, which means "prejudice or hatred against the Jewish people and/or things that are Jewish." This spirit proceeds from the mouth of the dragon, from Satan himself. Satan has always hated the Jewish people and things that are Jewish, because "salvation comes from the Jews" (John 4:22)

2. **Anti-Zionism**, which is the idea that all peoples have a right to their own land, except the Jewish people. This spirit proceeds from the mouth of the beast, the political world system, led by the antichrist. No politician will say that he is anti-Semitic. They diguise their Jew-hatred by saying that they only are against the state of Israel.

3. **Replacement Theology**, which is the teaching that the Jewish people were once God's people, but have been replaced, either by the church or by Islam. God's promises to Israel no longer apply. This spirit proceeds from the mouth of the false prophet and an unholy alliance between Islam and apostate Christianity.

All these evil spirits bring false and lying accusations against Israel to try to wipe out the land. It says that these three evil spirits "do signs" to gather the kings and leaders of the earth against Israel. This does not mean demonic signs and miracles. The Greek word used for "sign" here is *seemeion*, which means: "that which makes one person or thing to stand out from others; identification mark." The same word is used in the Gospel of Matthew, when Judas betrayed Jesus in Gethsemane.

> "While he was still speaking, Judas came, one of the twelve, and with him a great crowd with swords and clubs, from the chief priests and the elders of the people. **Now the betrayer had given them a sign**, saying, 'The one I will kiss is the

man; seize him.' And he came up to Jesus at once and said, 'Greetings, Rabbi!' And he kissed him." (Matt 26:47-49)

The sign Judas did was that he marked Jesus with a kiss to separate him from the others, so that he could be arrested. The three demons in Revelation 16 will go out to the "kings" of the earth in the last days and single out Israel as the target of all the devil's accusations, so that these leaders will be mobilized to march together against Israel. Anti-Semitism means treating Israel with a different standard than other countries. Israel is singled out and distinguished from other nations. John writes that, "the whole world lies in the power of the evil one" (1 Jn 5:19) and this is exactly what is happening today in for instance the UN.

The end time battle for the truth is here! The forces of anti-Semitism, anti-Zionism and replacement theology unite today in a final attack to strike Israel. These forces prepare the way for the final battle at Armageddon, when both Jews and born again Christians that are grafted into Israel's olive tree[39] will be attacked. We need to learn how to fight with the weapons that are mighty through God to demolish strongholds in the form of arguments that rebel against Him. To be able to do that, we must stand firmly anchored in the truth of God's Word.

> "For though we live in the world, we do not wage war as the world does. The weapons we fight with are not the weapons of the world. On the contrary, they have divine power to demolish strongholds. We demolish arguments and every pretension that sets itself up against the knowledge of God, and we take captive every thought to make it obedient to Christ." (2 Cor 10:3-5 NIV)

---

39   Cf. Rom 11:17; Rev 12:17.

LOVE THE TRUTH

Paul writes about the antichrist:

> "The coming of the lawless one is by the activity of Satan with all power and false signs and wonders, and with all wicked deception for those who are perishing, because they refused to love the truth and so be saved. Therefore God sends them a strong delusion, so that they may believe what is false, in order that all may be condemned who did not believe the truth but had pleasure in unrighteousness." (2 Thess 2:9–12)

If we do not believe the truth of God's Word and love it, we will be deceived by the devil's cunning lies and propaganda. In fact, we will not stand a chance to be able to defend ourselves against them. This is extremely serious and the only thing that can save us is the Word of God. Paul continues:

> "But we ought always to give thanks to God for you, brothers beloved by the Lord, **because God chose you as the firstfruits to be saved, through sanctification by the Spirit and belief in the truth.** To this he called you through our gospel, so that you may obtain the glory of our Lord Jesus Christ. So then, brothers, **stand firm** and hold to the traditions that you were taught by us, either by our spoken word or by our letter." (2 Thess 2:13-15)

It is also written in the book of Hebrews, "Therefore we must pay much closer attention to what we have heard, lest we drift away from it." (Heb 2:1) We need to stand firm in the truth of the Word of God. God's Word is our only security and the only thing that can show us the way. "Your word is a lamp to my feet and a light to my path." (Ps 119:105) The spiritual battle for truth will become extremely intense in the end times. That is why it is necessary that we daily read the Bible during prayer and study the Scriptures as much as we possibly can.

Jesus promised, "When the Spirit of truth comes, he will guide you into all the truth, for he will not speak on his own authority, but whatever he hears he will speak, and he will declare to you the things that are to come." (Jn 16:13) "But the Helper, the Holy Spirit, whom the Father will send in my name, he will teach you all things and bring to your remembrance all that I have said to you." (Jn 14:26)

It is also important that we read **the entire** Bible. It says, "**All Scripture** is breathed out by God and profitable for teaching, for reproof, for correction, and for training in righteousness." (2 Tim 3:16) And also, "The **sum** of your word is truth." (Ps 119:160) **If we are not reading the whole Bible we don't get the whole truth!** Peter wrote, "And we have the prophetic word more fully confirmed, to which you will do well to pay attention as to a lamp shining in a dark place, until the day dawns and the morning star rises in your hearts" (2 Pe 1:19) We do not stand a chance to find the right way in this dark and troubled time, if we do not carefully study the prophetic word.

It is a good and proven habit to read through the entire Bible every year. Just as we need to eat physical food every day, we also need to read the Bible every day. "It is written: Man does not live by bread alone, but by every word that proceeds from the mouth of God." (Matt 4:4)

The king of Israel was commanded to read God's Word every day to learn to fear God and obey Him (Deut 17:18-19). This included King David and the world's wisest man King Solomon, who wrote parts of the Bible themselves. How much more do we need to read the Bible every day to learn to fear God and obey him?

This world bombards us every day with information about all sorts of things. We need to prioritize the Word of God more than all other information, so that we do not adapt to the world's way of thinking and acting. "Do not be conformed to this world, but be transformed by the renewal of your mind, that by testing you may discern what is the will of God, what is good and acceptable and perfect." (Rom 12:2)

It is even a command to study God's Word. "You shall love the Lᴏʀᴅ your God with all your heart and with all your soul and with all your might. And these words that I command you today shall be on your heart. You shall teach them diligently to your children, and shall talk of them when you sit in your house, and when you walk by the way, and when you lie down, and when you rise." (Deut 6:5-7) We are commanded to love God above all things by putting His words on our hearts and speaking of them every day!

Everyone has the same amount of time to use! The question is how we prioritize our time. The very best is without a doubt to **read** God's Word. If you don't always have time to read the Bible, you can listen to the Bible on your phone. We need to become "readers" again and read the Bible more than we listen to preaching and teaching.

> "Oh how I love your law! It is my meditation all the day. Your commandment makes me wiser than my enemies, for it is ever with me. I have more understanding than all my teachers, for your testimonies are my meditation." (Ps 119:97–99)

We cannot always prevent lies and accusations from being spread about Israel. But we can and we must learn to fight the lies with the help of the Word of God! The world will not always listen to us. But especially the church should know the truth and stand up for it. The congregation is "the pillar and foundation of the truth" (1 Tim. 3:15) and we are called to be salt and light.

CHAPTER 6
THE FUTURE OF THE LAND

"For thus said the LORD of hosts, after his glory sent me to the nations who plundered you, for he who touches you touches the apple of his eye: 'Behold, I will shake my hand over them, and they shall become plunder for those who served them.' Then you will know that the LORD of hosts has sent me. Sing and rejoice, O daughter of Zion, for behold, I come and I will dwell in your midst, declares the LORD. And many nations shall join themselves to the LORD in that day, and shall be my people. And I will dwell in your midst, and you shall know that the LORD of hosts has sent me to you. And the LORD will inherit Judah as his portion in the holy land, and will again choose Jerusalem." —Zecheriah 2:8–12

God calls the Land of Israel his own Land. Ezekiel describes in chapters 35 and 36 the special anger God feels towards those who take the Land away from his people.

"Because you cherished perpetual enmity and gave over the people of Israel to the power of the sword at the time of their calamity, at the time of their final punishment, therefore, as I live, declares the Lord GOD, I will prepare you for blood, and blood shall pursue you; because you did not hate bloodshed, therefore blood shall pursue you. ... **Because you said, 'These two nations and these two countries shall be mine, and we will take possession of them'**—although the LORD was there— therefore, as I live, declares the Lord GOD, I will deal with you according to the anger and envy that you showed because of your hatred against them. And I will make myself known among them, when I judge you. And you shall know that I am the LORD. I have heard all the revilings that you uttered against the mountains of Israel, saying, 'They are laid desolate; they are given us to devour.'" (Eze 35:5–6; 10–12)

Notice that this is specifically talking about the "mountains of Israel." "I have heard all the revilings that you uttered against the mountains of Israel, saying, 'They are laid desolate; they are given us to devour.'" 80% of the Mountains of Israel lie within the area that the world community today calls the "West Bank" which they want to take from the Jewish people, to establish a Palestinian state there.

Ezekiel continues to prophesy of this area:

"Son of man, prophesy to the mountains of Israel and say, 'Mountains of Israel, hear the word of the LORD. This is what the Sovereign LORD says: The enemy said of you, "Aha! The ancient heights have become our possession.' Therefore prophesy and say, 'This is what the Sovereign LORD says: Because they ravaged and crushed you from every side so that you became the possession of the rest of the nations and the object of people's malicious talk and slander, therefore, mountains of Israel, hear the word of the Sovereign LORD: This is what the Sovereign LORD says to the mountains and hills, to the ravines and valleys, to the desolate ruins and the deserted towns that have been plundered and ridiculed by the rest of the nations around you— this is what the Sovereign LORD says: In my burning zeal I have spoken against the rest of the nations, and against all Edom, for **with glee and with malice in their hearts they made my land their own possession so that they might plunder its pastureland.**" (Eze 36:1–5 NIV)

The prophetic words in the Bible are so incredibly accurate. 2,500 years ago, Ezekiel prophesied about the inhabitants of the Mountains of Israel: "the object of people's malicious talk and slander." There is probably no one today who is as slandered and mocked by the media and politicians as the so-called "settlers", i.e. the Jews who live on the Mountains of Israel, despite the fact that the entire international community gave them the right to settle there only a hundred years ago. According to data from 2023, there are 850,000 Jews living in these disputed areas—Judea and Samaria.[40]

Note that the Lord says about the Jews who live on the Mountains of Israel and who provoke the whole world, that they live in "My land." It is written about Israel's enemies, "with glee and with malice in their hearts they made **My land** their own possession so that they might plunder its pastureland." God calls the "West Bank", the area that has been called Judea and Samaria throughout history since the days of the Bible, for **His** land. Today the politicians in the world want to empty God's own land of all Jews. No wonder it arouses the wrath of God!

Ezekiel continues to prophesy about what will happen to this area:

---

40 There are 502,991 Jewish residents in Judea and Samaria as of January 1, 2023 according to a document that drew data from the Israeli Interior Ministry population register. This does not include the almost 350,000 Jews who live in the eastern part of Jerusalem ("Jewish population in Judea and Samaria tops half a million," *JNS,* Feb 2, 2023, *https://jns.org/jewish-population-in-judea-and-sa-maria-tops-half-a- million* [Dec 22, 2023]).

"Therefore prophesy concerning the land of Israel, and say to the mountains and hills, to the ravines and valleys, Thus says the Lord GOD: **Behold, I have spoken in my jealous wrath, because you have suffered the reproach of the nations.** Therefore thus says the Lord GOD: I swear that the nations that are all around you shall themselves suffer reproach.

But you, O mountains of Israel, shall shoot forth your branches and yield your fruit to my people Israel, for they will soon come home. For behold, I am for you, and I will turn to you, and you shall be tilled and sown. **And I will multiply people on you, the whole house of Israel, all of it.** The cities shall be inhabited and the waste places rebuilt. And I will multiply on you man and beast, and they shall multiply and be fruitful. And I will cause you to be inhabited as in your former times, and will do more good to you than ever before. Then you will know that I am the LORD. I will let people walk on you, even my people Israel. And they shall possess you, and you shall be their inheritance, and you shall no longer bereave them of children." (Eze 36:6–12)

God gathers His people from the four corners of the earth to stay particularly on the Mountains of Israel. The LORD says: "And I will multiply people on you, the whole house of Israel, all of it. The cities shall be inhabited and the waste places rebuilt. And I will multiply on you man and beast, and they shall multiply and be fruitful." (36:10–11) This is happening right before our eyes, despite the opposition of the whole world! Shiloh, Ophrah, Ephrat, Bethel are just a few among many examples of ancient biblical cities that have layed in ruins for millennia, but are now being rebuilt, just as God said. No wonder the enemy rages.

The end result will be good for the Mountains of Israel, "And I will not let you hear anymore the reproach of the nations, and you shall no longer bear the disgrace of the peoples and no longer cause your nation to stumble, declares the Lord GOD." (36:15) On the other hand, Israel's enemies will be despised: "Therefore prophesy concerning the land of Israel, and say to the mountains and hills, to the ravines and valleys, Thus says the Lord GOD: Behold, I have spoken in my jealous wrath, because you have suffered the reproach of the nations. Therefore thus says the Lord GOD: I swear that the nations that are all around you shall themselves suffer reproach." (36:6–7)

ISRAEL'S FUTURE BORDERS

There are several different descriptions of the borders of Israel in the Bible. The first and largest area is that which was given to Abraham in Genesis 15:18–21. It includes the entire area between Egypt and the Euphrates River. Israel has never occupied all of this territory, but it will take place in the Messianic age when the kingdom is restored to Israel. Jesus said, "For truly, I say to you, until heaven and earth pass away, not an iota, not a dot, will pass from the Law until all is accomplished." (Mt 5:18). The promise that Abraham received will be fulfilled.

The second description of Israel's borders covers the area that God promised through Moses in Numbers 34:1-15, when the children of Israel were ready to enter the Land. This area is smaller and it eventually fell to Israel under King Solomon. The area that Joshua distributed in Joshua 13–19 was smaller than the area in Numbers 34. It took over 400 years before Israel could take possession of that entire area. The area that the Jews received after the captivity in Babylon and that existed during the time of Jesus was even smaller.

Moses explained to Israel:

> "And if the LORD your God enlarges your territory, as he has sworn to your fathers, and gives you all the land that he promised to give to your fathers— provided you are careful to keep all this commandment, which I command you to-

day, by loving the LORD your God and by walking ever in his ways." (Deut 19:8-9)

In other words, the borders of Israel vary depending on the obedience of the children of Israel and their relationship to God. This has also been the case in modern times since the state of Israel was formed in 1948, when they only received half of the Land, west of the Jordan River. Therefore, it is important that the Jewish people repent to Him and obey His commandments. "Righteousness exalts a nation, but sin is a reproach to any people." (Prov 14:34)

In the future, at the final restoration, the sages of Israel declare that the whole earth will belong to Israel.

> "In the future the land of Israel will expand and occupy every country on earth. The Temple Mount will be as the Holy of Holiest, all Jerusalem will be as the Temple Mount, all Israel will be like Jerusalem and the whole world like Israel" (*Pesikta Rabbati*).[41]

This is also in line with what Paul writes about Abraham that he was promised **the whole world** by God, "For the promise to Abraham and his offspring that he would be **heir of the world** did not come through the law but through the righteousness of faith." (Rom 4:13) Jesus promised, "Blessed are the meek, for they shall inherit the earth." (Matt 5:5) In Acts, the apostles call the Messianic kingdom of God on earth "the kingdom restored to Israel." "Lord, will you at this time restore the kingdom to Israel?" (Acts 1:6) This is the kingdom that all the prophets spoke of, with Jerusalem, "the city of the great King," as the capital.

---

41 Cf. Adam Eliyahu Berkowitz, "Jewish Prophecy: In Coming Messianic Era, Israel's Borders Will Encompass the World," *Israel365 News* (June 8, 2016), https://israel365news.com/307912/global-kingdom-israel-times-messiah/#Q8GzqK5W8YWsKSfd.99 [Dec 22, 2023].

King David prayed:

> "Therefore you are great, O Lᴏʀᴅ God. For there is none like you, and there is no God besides you, according to all that we have heard with our ears. . And who is like your people Israel, the one nation on earth whom God went to redeem to be his people, making himself a name and doing for them great and awesome things by driving out before your people, whom you redeemed for yourself from Egypt, a nation and its gods? And you established for yourself your people Israel to be your people forever. And you, O Lᴏʀᴅ, became their God. And now, O Lᴏʀᴅ God, confirm forever the word that you have spoken concerning your servant and concerning his house, and **do as you have spoken. And your name will be magnified forever, saying, 'The Lᴏʀᴅ of hosts is God over Israel.'**" (2 Sam 7:25–26)

God wants to use the church to bless Israel. We are involved in a spiritual battle for the truth, where we do not fight against people of flesh and blood, "but against the rulers, against the authorities, against the cosmic powers over this present darkness, against the spiritual forces of evil in the heavenly places." (Eph 6:12). Paul continues in Ephesians:

> "Therefore take up the whole armor of God, that you may be able to withstand in the evil day, and having done all, to stand firm. Stand therefore, having fastened on the belt of truth, and having put on the breastplate of righteousness, and, as shoes for your feet, having put on the readiness given by the gospel of peace. In all circumstances take up the shield of faith, with which you can extinguish all the flaming darts of the evil one; and take the helmet of salvation, and the sword of the Spirit, which is the word of God, praying at all times in the Spirit, with all prayer and supplica-

tion. To that end, keep alert with all perseverance, making supplication for all the saints." (Eph 6:13–18)

All the saints also include Israel which is a holy people. We are involved in an intense spiritual battle for the restoration of Israel. It is a battle for the truth. God has promised that those who bless Israel, He will bless. But those who curse, literally "belittle" in Hebrew, God Himself will curse.

"Now the LORD said to Abram, "Go from your country[b] and your kindred and your father's house to the land that I will show you. And I will make of you a great nation, and I will bless you and make your name great, so that you will be a blessing. I will bless those who bless you, and him who dishonors you I will curse, and in you all the families of the earth shall be blessed." (Gen 12:1–3)

Today we are in desperate need of God's blessing both as a church and as a nation. God will not be able to fully bless a church that does not bless Israel.

In the spiritual struggle for the salvation of Israel, the church must remember:

1. **We need to be prepared to fight for the truth, faithful unto death.** "For I am already being poured out as a drink offering, and the time of my departure has come. I have fought the good fight, I have finished the race, I have kept the faith. Henceforth there is laid up for me the crown of righteousness, which the Lord, the righteous judge, will award to me on that day, and not only to me but also to all who have loved his appearing." (2 Tim 4:6–8)

2. **We need to learn to fight together as an army in love and unity.** "For as in one body we have many members, and the

members do not all have the same function, so we, though many, are one body in Christ, and individually members one of another. Having gifts that differ according to the grace given to us" (Rom 12:4–6)

3. **We need to be rooted and founded in the truth from the Word of God.** "Stand therefore, having fastened on the belt of truth" (Eph 6:14)

4. **We need to pray daily for Israel.** "On your walls, O Jerusalem, I have set watchmen; all the day and all the night they shall never be silent. You who put the LORD in remembrance, take no rest, and give him no rest until he establishes Jerusalem and makes it a praise in the earth." (Isa 62:6–7)

5. **We need to boldly proclaim the truth in the Word of God.** "and take ... the sword of the Spirit, which is the word of God" (Eph 6:17)

6. **We need wisdom to be able to warn as many as possible, especially among leaders.** "Now therefore, O kings, be wise; be warned, O rulers of the earth. ... Kiss the Son, lest he be angry, and you perish in the way, for his wrath is quickly kindled. Blessed are all who take refuge in him." (Ps 2:10, 12)

7. **We need strong prophetic voices that can warn.** "Son of man, I have made you a watchman for the house of Israel. Whenever you hear a word from my mouth, you shall give them warning from me." (Eze 3:17)

8. **We need to have the same comittment to Israel as Ruth the Moabitess had.** "But Ruth said, 'Do not urge me to leave you or to return from following you. For where you go I will go, and where you lodge I will lodge. Your people shall be my peo-

ple, and your God my God. Where you die I will die, and there will I be buried. May the LORD do so to me and more also if anything but death parts me from you." (Ruth 1:16–17)

CHAPTER 7
THE FUTURE OF GAZA

As I am writing the last chapter of this book in November, 2023, Israel is at war in Gaza against the terrorist organization Hamas. On October 7, 2023, approximately 3,000 Hamas terrorists made their way, together with a number of civilians from Gaza, over the border into Israel and murdered over 1,200 people, of which about 1,000 were civilians. Hamas gleefully filmed themselves raping them, mutilating them, burning them alive, and committing bestial crimes. Furthermore, they took over 240 civilians, including women, children, and the elderly, into Gaza as hostages. It is the worst catastrophe that has befallen the Jewish people since the Holocaust. Hamas has also fired over 10,000 rockets at civilian targets in Israel. Inside Gaza, Hamas uses the civilian population as human shields. All these acts constitute serious war crimes. Despite this, thousands of people have marched in the streets all over the world in support of Hamas. It is unimaginable! Israel has mobilized almost 400,000 troops and entered Gaza to once and for all wipe out Hamas as a terrorist organization. The whole world is now wondering what will happen to Gaza after Hamas is defeated. Does God have anything to say in his Word about this?

It is remarkable that there is an entire chapter in the Bible that seems to describe exactly what is happening in Gaza. We need to study this chapter and take to heart the prophetic promises about Gaza so that the church can act accordingly.

A PROPHETIC DREAM

I want to relate a prophetic dream that Tim Hostetter, an intercessor and friend in the United States, had in the beginning of December 2022—in other words, almost one year before the Hamas massacre on October 7, 2023. This is important in order to emphasize that God is in full control of what is happening right now.[42]

> "On December 4, 2022, I dreamt that I was talking on the phone with a dear Israeli friend of mine. He told me there is a move of the Holy Spirit stirring in Israel. I knew there was a sense of security that had been removed from Israel as a judgment of God. It was like Biblical times when bad things would start to happen, but it would lead to a move of national repentance and return to obeying God's commandments in the Torah (as in the book of Judges, for example).

> "My friend said that the way to 'push it through' in prayer (this work of God's Spirit in Israel), was by using the promises in Scripture, like a person who labored until sunrise. In the dream, the Biblical example may have been about Rachel when she gave birth to Benjamin (Gen 35:16–18), or one of the other Matriarchs. The theme being communicated was about Biblical stories of Jewish people not giving up on God's mercy.

> "In the dream, I thought of a Scripture where God said, "My holy people have become drunkards and prostitutes." (I don't think such a Scripture literally exists—but this theme is certainly present in the Bible, especially in the Prophets.) It was so painful to feel God's heart, and I was weeping and

---

42 The description of the dream comes from personal correspondence; minor clarifications added.

weeping because of the situation of sin and judgment. **However, I knew that it would result in a move of repentance that would happen in Israel. And I knew that a sense of security would be restored.**

"In the dream I knew that I was going to be sharing publicly with a Christian audience who wanted to be praying for Israel. **I knew that this was the next prophetic word we needed to be praying into: that Israel would repent and return to Torah, just like in the Bible stories.**

"I wanted Christians to understand, for the sake of prayer, that this call to repentance was about Jews living righteously according to God's commandments in the Torah. I wanted them to know this, so that when it was happening, they would be encouraged in their prayers for Israel. I knew that belief in Jesus might not happen in this move of the Spirit— but that the repentance and resulting mercy was still going to be real. I felt that believers needed to have understanding about this, so that they would continue praying for Israel and not be disappointed that mass belief in Yeshua had not happened yet.

"During this dream, I was driving with my wife past a place where we rarely ever go. We were alone in the car. In real life, a couple weeks ago, we happened to drive past that place together, and we were alone in the car. I wondered if that was a sign that the timing for this dream was **now**."

Hostetter's described his most important impressions from the dream:

"It seems that God has planned a time of shaking for Israel because of a move of the Holy Spirit which He has planned for her. This is a move of repentance and returning to God's commandments in the Torah. We must pray fervently, not giving up on God's mercy, in order to see this move of the Spirit happen.

"Many believers need to be encouraged that Israel's repentance and return to Torah is a legitimate move of God (Eze 36:24–28). This understanding is necessary so that those who interceede will stay steadfast in prayer."

"I will take you from the nations and gather you from all the countries and bring you into your own land. I will sprinkle clean water on you, and you shall be clean from all your uncleannesses, and from all your idols I will cleanse you. And I will give you a new heart, and a new spirit I will put within you. And I will remove the heart of stone from your flesh and give you a heart of flesh. And **I will put my Spirit within you, and cause you to walk in my statutes and be careful to obey my rules.** You shall dwell in the land that I gave to your fathers, and you shall be my people, and I will be your God." (Eze 36:24–28)

REFLECTIONS ON THE DREAM

Tim got this dream almost a full year in advance. Two weeks before the massacre on October 7, he drove in his car past the place he had seen in the dream and wondered if the time had come for the fulfillment.

The dream was about Israel needing to turn from lawlessness to a life in righteousness in obedience to the covenant and the commandments of God. During the last year, the secular sector of society in Israel have rebelled against religious and God-fearing Jews in the Land in increasingly serious ways. On the Day of Atonement 2023, the holiest day of the year, in several places, especially in Tel Aviv, they even began to physically attack those who had gathered to pray outdoors. The mayor in Tel Aviv declared that Tel Aviv is a secular city and those who do not accept that, need to move elsewhere. In other words, God-fearing Jews are not welcome to live in places of their own choosing in their own country! Over the past year, many have begun to fear a civil war.

According to the dream, as an act of judgment, God would remove the sense of safety from Israel, which is exactly what happened when Hamas attacked Israel on October 7. Everything that Israel trusted in—the army, the security establishment, the new high-tech security barrier to Gaza, etc. Everything failed! Safety disappeared.

God would allow something difficult to happen to Israel, just like when they fell away from God in the book of Judges and came under oppression from the enemy. It says, for example, "And the people of Israel again did what was evil in the sight of the LORD, and the LORD strengthened Eglon the king of Moab against Israel, because they had done what was evil in the sight of the LORD." (Judges 3:12) The Lord **strengthened Eglon, the king of Moab, against Israel,** when Israel fell away from him. The whole world, and above all Israel, were shocked on October 7 by Hamas's strength and ability to overcome all of Israel's proud defenses at the border to Gaza in a single moment. No one had expected it. Israel's enemies around the world have been celebrating this triumph ever since.

It is true that the righteous often suffer injustice and persecution in this life. And one cannot make pronouncements about individual cases as Job's friends did. At the same time, from a collective perspective, one must be able to take the teaching of Scripture seriously, that when the covenant people of God openly reject faithfulness to the covenant, they also leave a certain measure of God's merciful protection.

One of the largest disasters on October 7, was the massive Nova festival in the wilderness, where over 360 people were murdered in one place. Nova can be compared to an Israeli "Burning Man," where people deliberately engage in lawlessness, with drugs, drunkenness, sexual immorality, and literal idolatrous statues. Furthermore, it was held exactly on a high holy Sabbath on God's calendar, the eighth day of the Feast of Tabernacles, when Israel celebrates the joy of God's Law. All God-fearing Jews were at home, or in synagogue. Thousands of young people had partied with trance music throughout the night, and many were still partying at 6:30 in the morning on October 7. Most of them were high on various drugs.

It is hard not to be reminded of the words from the dream, "My holy people have become drunkards and prostitutes."

It can also be noted that the kibbutz that suffered the worst during the massacre, is known as the most secular kibbutz in Israel. Similarly, Hamas fired most of its rockets toward the LGBTQ movement's capital, Tel Aviv, not against Jerusalem. There was a noticeable difference.

After little more than three weeks from October 7, the Israeli army freed the first of the hostages from Hamas, a female soldier named Ori Magidish. Even though her family didn't seem to be very religious, they had immediately begun to cry out to God for her deliverance. The first thing they did was to get a Torah scroll (the five books of Moses), Israel's covenant with God, which they carried into the daughter's room while they called out to God: "Just as we brought this Torah into Ori's room, may you soon bring our daughter back home unharmed to us!" Thus the parents showed enormous love and joy for the Law and the miracle did not fail to arrive. God answered their prayers!

Ori means "My light." It says: "Your word is a lamp to my feet and a light to my path" (Ps 119:105) Can God speak more plainly? Ori's mother's fervent prayers and tears to God for her daughter's release were also captured on video, and the testimony of the family's turn to godliness and prayer has been noticed throughout Israel, even in the Knesset, as an example for the entire country. God is speaking clearly to all in Israel who have ears to hear.

The prophetic dream has begun to be fulfilled, as many secular Israelis have started to turn to God. Those who have never celebrated Sabbath before are baking challah bread in honor of God's special day. The one thing that has been most in demand among Israeli soldiers since the war broke out, has been the tassels which God commanded his people to wear in the corners of their garments to remember all the commandments of the Law.

> "The LORD said to Moses, 'Speak to the people of Israel, and tell them to make tassels on the corners of their garments throughout their generations, and to put a cord of blue on the tassel of each corner. **And it shall be a tassel for you to look at and remember all the commandments of the LORD, to do them, not to follow after your own heart and your own eyes, which you are inclined to whore after.** So you shall remember and do all my commandments, and be holy to your God. I am the LORD your God, who brought you out of the land of Egypt to be your God: I am the LORD your God.'" (Num 15:37–41)

Tens of thousands of secular Jews who had never used them before have begun to wear these tassels in repentance and a turning away from lawlessness, just as in the prophetic dream. This is a work of the Holy Spirit.

It is remarkable to see that in the Hebrew text of Numbers 15:39 it literally says: "And it shall be a tassel for you to look at **him** and remember all the commandments of the Lord, to do them, not to follow after your own heart and your own eyes, which you are inclined to whore after." In Hebrew, the word tassel is a feminine word. But here it actually says "when you see **him**" with reference to the tassels. It is a clear prophecy of the Messiah who is the Word. **The turning away from lawlessness to obedience to God's commandments is the first phase of Israel's salvation through the Messiah.** When Messiah finally reveals himself to Israel, they will say just as the first disciples said: "We have found him of whom Moses in the Law and also the prophets wrote, Jesus of Nazareth, the son of Joseph." (Jn 1:45) Paul explains, "So the law became our guardian [lit. pedagogue] to lead us to Messiah." (Gal 3:24 BSB)

In the dream, Tim experienced that we need to enter into persistent battle in prayer for the salvation of Israel until a new day dawns, just as when Jacob struggled with God! "And Jacob was left alone. And a man wrestled with him until the breaking of the day ... The sun rose upon him as he passed Penuel" (Gen 32:24, 31). What is happening now in Israel is a prelude to the Gog and Magog war and Jacob's trouble described in Jeremiah 30. Micah prophesied:

> "Therefore he shall give them up until the time when she who is in labor has given birth; then the rest of his brothers shall return to the people of Israel. And he shall stand and shepherd his flock in the strength of the LORD, in the majesty of the name of the LORD his God. And they shall dwell secure, for now he shall be great to the ends of the earth." (Mica 5:3–4)

PRAY FOR THE ARABS IN GAZA

We also need to pray for the Arabs in Gaza. They have suffered immensely under Hamas' wicked terror regime in Gaza, which they themselves have largely supported over the years. Shortly after Israel began entering Gaza, Hamas leader Ismail Haniyeh, who has a fortune valued at $4 billion and lives in a luxury hotel in Qatar, said: "We need to see more blood from [our] women and children so that the will to fight increases among our soldiers." He then ordered all civilians in Gaza not to flee to safety, but to stay and sacrifice their lives to Allah as living shields for the terrorists. Hamas has murdered scores of Palestinian Arabs that tried to escape to safety in southern Gaza. Images of dead bodies, including children, lying on the road to the

South in Gaza are circulating on the Internet. Hamas blames Israel, but closer studies show that Hamas is behind it.

Mothers in Gaza have begun to raise their voices in disgust at Hamas. The best thing Israel can do is to liberate not only Israel, but also the Arabs in Gaza from Hamas. They suffer terribly under Hamas and under the perverted ideology that Hamas is an expression of. Gaza needs revival, they need bold preachers who proclaim the Gospel. There has been a report from CBN[43] about Jesus appearing in dreams to over 200 Palestinian men in Gaza, who are now seeking guidance on how to follow him. God also loves the sons of Ishmael!

WHAT DOES THE BIBLE SAY ABOUT GAZA?

Jesus said, "Heaven and earth will pass away, but my words will not pass away." (Matt 24:35) And King David wrote, "Forever, O LORD, your word is firmly fixed in the heavens." (Ps 119:89) "Let all the earth fear the LORD; let all the inhabitants of the world stand in awe of him! For he spoke, and it came to be; he commanded, and it stood firm. The LORD brings the counsel of the nations to nothing; he frustrates the plans of the peoples. The counsel of the LORD stands forever, the plans of his heart to all generations." (Ps 33:8–11) We will now look at what the Word of God has to say about Gaza and its future.

The first thing we need to establish is that Gaza is a part of God's own Land. It talks specifically about the inheritance that Joshua was commanded to distribute to the tribe of Judah:

> "The allotment for the tribe of the people of Judah according to their clans ... Ekron, with its towns and its villages; from Ekron to the sea, all that were by the side of Ashdod, with their villages. Ashdod, its towns and its villages; **Gaza,**

---

43 "Jesus Reportedly Appearing to Palestinians in Gaza," *CBN News*, Feb 17, 2024, *https://youtu.be/2AVBzmuY8fQ?* [March 22, 2024].

its towns and its villages; to the Brook of Egypt, and the Great Sea with its coastline." (Jos 15:1, 45–47)

Gaza is, in other words, a part of the promised land that was given to Israel forever. It is important to have this as a basis when we seek the will of God to be done in Israel and Gaza. It is written:

> "He is the LORD our God; his judgments are in all the earth. He remembers his covenant forever, the word that he commanded, for a thousand generations, the covenant that he made with Abraham, his sworn promise to Isaac, which he confirmed to Jacob as a statute, to Israel as an everlasting covenant, saying, 'To you I will give the land of Canaan as your portion for an inheritance.'" (Ps 105:7–11)

The main question that is now being debated among politicians all over the world, is what will happen to Gaza when Hamas is defeated. The entire international community, led by the United States and Joe Biden, want to see a two-state solution established. They want the Palestinian Authority under Mahmoud Abbas, to take over Gaza and the whole world is putting pressure on Israel to now realise the "two-state solution." This would only prolong the conflict.

God has another solution for Gaza that we can read about in Zechariah 9. According to ancient Jewish commentaries, this chapter talks specifically about the restoration and severe trials during the last generations, before the coming of the Messiah. All the five actors involved in the ongoing war that have attacked Israel thus far are mentioned in this chapter: Syria, Lebanon, Gaza, Yemen and the "Palestinian" Arabs.

In this chapter, Israel is promised victory over all the five surrounding enemies. The road to restoration is not always straight. How the promises are fulfilled depends a lot on the prayers of the believers, whether this happens right now, or in the near future. Jesus brings out this concept in his final eschatological speech, where he says:

"Pray that your flight may not be in winter or on a Sabbath." (Matt 24:20) That is to say, within the context of the fulfillment of the prophetic word, circumstances can be improved or worsened, depending on the prayers of God's people.

ZECHARIAH CHAPTER 9

"The oracle of the word of the LORD is against the land of Hadrach and Damascus is its resting place. For the LORD has an eye on mankind and on all the tribes of Israel." (Zec 9:1)

Chapter 9 of Zechariah begins a new section of prophecies. From this chapter to the end of Zechariah, there are no more personal or direct historical references in the prophecies. We will now study each verse in this interesting chapter. We will also quote one-thousand, sometimes two-thousand-year-old Jewish commentaries on these verses which speak of what is happening right now in Gaza and Israel.

According to an ancient Jewish commentary on verse 1 by Rav Yehudah bar Ilai, who was born year 100 in Galilee, this entire chapter of Zechariah talks about "the time of restoration and severe trials that will take place in the last generations just before the coming of the Messiah." He supports this with the understanding of the expression "land of Hadrach." Hadrach is only mentioned in this verse in the entire Bible. According to Rav Yehudah, Hadrach is not the name of a city or a geographical area but a reference to the Messiah. Hadrach is composed of two Hebrew words *had*, meaning sharp, and *rach*, meaning soft. The foremost Jewish Bible commentator in history, Rashi (who lived in France, 1040–1105) quotes Rav Yehudah in his commentary on this verse, "This is a reference to the Messiah who is harsh with the nations but gentle with Israel."

As we mentioned earlier, all the actors in today's conflict with Israel are mentioned in this chapter: Syria, Lebanon with Hezbollah, Gaza with Hamas, the Arabs in Judea and Samaria (the so-called West Bank), and even Yemen, which has also begun to attack Israel!

Damascus is mentioned first, located in Syria. Damascus has been in focus as a theater of war in the current conflict for more than 10 years. In 2006, Iran and Syria entered into a joint agreement on military cooperation, making Syria a conflict zone for Israel, because of Iran's proxy forces. Especially after the "Arab Spring" which began in 2011, Israel has carried out hundreds of bombing raids into Syria against Iranian interests. After the Hamas massacre on October 7, this battle zone also heated up, and rocket fire started from Syria into Israel.

"For the LORD has an eye on mankind and on all the tribes of Israel." The Jewish scholar Radak (Rabbi David Kimhi who lived in France 1160-1235) translates this as follows, "All eyes will be directed towards God and all the tribes of Israel." This is indeed true after what happened October 7, when Israel is ever more in focus of the whole world. God will get everyone's attention through the conflict with Israel! It also says about the end times in Zechariah 12:2, "Behold, I am about to make Jerusalem a cup of staggering to all the surrounding peoples."

Hamas called the massacre on October 7, "The Al-Aqsa Flood". Al-Aqsa is the name of the Muslim Mosque on the Temple Mount in Jerusalem. Jerusalem is the focus of the entire conflict.

LEBANON IS ALSO A PART

> "...and on Hamath also, which borders on it, Tyre and Sidon, though they are very wise. Tyre has built herself a rampart and heaped up silver like dust, and fine gold like the mud of the streets. But behold, the Lord will strip her of her possessions and strike down her power on the sea, and she shall be devoured by fire." (Zec 9:2-4)

The prophecy continues and begins to touch on Lebanon. Tyre and Sidon are main strongholds for the terrorist organization Hezbollah. "Tyre has built herself a rampart and heaped up silver like dust, and fine gold like the mud of the streets." Hezbollah is the world's richest and most powerful terrorist organization. They boast of being able to field an army of 100,000 trained warriors. They have become extremely rich through Iran's billions over several decades, as well as through drug smuggling, primarily in Latin America. Hezbollah constitutes a state within the state of Lebanon. Their army is larger than Lebanon's army and corresponds to an average Arab state's army. They have 150,000 rockets in their arsenal,[44] which is more than most countries in the world possess.

"But behold, the Lord will strip her of her possessions and strike down her power on the sea, and she shall be devoured by fire." Rabbi Mahari Kara (Joseph ben Simeon Kara who lived ca. 1065-1135) comments on this verse: "Tyre have built a firm stronghold to protect themselves against the Jewish people." Rashi and Radak add, "and have boasted that she will never be defeated." These almost thousand-year-old comments on this prophecy give an incredibly accurate description of Hezbollah's arrogance and self-confidence today, above all through statements of its leader Hassan Nasrallah. Rashi and Radak continue: "but it won't help her." Rabbi Ibn Ezra who lived in Spain 1089–1167 comments further: "God will let Israel inherit her."

"The Lord will strip her of her possessions and strike down her power on the sea." This can also be translated: "and he will knock down her wealth with the help of the sea." Immediately after the massacre on October 7, when Israel declared war on Hamas, many feared that Hezbollah would also enter the conflict with its 150,000 missiles, many of which, unlike Hamas' rockets, are precision-guided and can reach most targets throughout Israel. However, the US immediately sent its largest warships to the area and positioned it off

---

44 Some recent estimates rise to 200,000 rockets (Maariv, "Hezbollah has up to 200,000 rockets aimed at Israel, INSS assesses," *Jerusalem Post*, Oct 23, 2023, https://www.jpost.com/middle-east/article-769639 [March 22, 2023]).

the coast of Lebanon. This certainly contributed to them not acting at that point. When Hezbollah announced that Nasrallah would give a big speech in front of thousands of Hezbollah adherants on November 3, many expected Nasrallah to declare war on Israel. He didn't. Instead, he directed his anger at the United States. It is quite possible that it was "with the help of the sea" in the form of the United States' largest warship stationed directly off the coast that deterred him.

"... and she shall be devoured by fire." Perhaps this is referring to Israeli bombing raids into Lebanon. Israel does not have a sufficiently effective defense against 150,000 rockets, if Hezbollah decides to deploy all of them against Israel. Therefore, as a deterrence, Israel has announced to both Hezbollah and Lebanon's government that if this happens, Israel's response will be to "bomb Lebanon back to the Stone Age." This would mean destroying the entire infrastructure of Lebanon, their electricity and water maintenance, sewage plants, etc., which will make Lebanon uninhabitable for a long time. Israel has already begun to respond to Hezbollah's deadly shelling into Israel—where several Israeli soldiers and civilians have died—with heavy fire into Lebanon.

THE FUTURE OF GAZA

"Ashkelon shall see it, and be afraid; Gaza too, and shall writhe in anguish; Ekron also, because its hopes are confounded. The king shall perish from Gaza; Ashkelon shall be uninhabited." (Zec 9:5)

Now the prophecy focuses on Gaza and the "Palestinian" Arabs. Ashkelon, Gaza and Ekron are all known cities where the Philistines lived in biblical times. The Philistines were Israel's worst enemies ever since the days of Samson. The Philistines are an extinct people who disappeared from the pages of history when Assyria took these cities and exiled the population. Today however, the spiritual successors of the Philistines, the "Palestinians" live in the region and have assumed both the Philistine name and role vis-à-vis Israel. These prophecies in the light of the coming of Messiah are definitely talking about them.

It says about them, when they see what happens to Tyre and Sidon, i.e Hezbollah: "Ashkelon shall see it, and be afraid; Gaza too, and shall writhe in anguish; Ekron also, because its hopes are confounded." This was actually what happened when Hezbollah didn't declare war on Israel. Especially after Nasrallah's speech on November 3, their hopes were dashed.

Then the prophecy continues by saying: "Gaza loses its king." It can also be translated: "A king shall perish in Gaza." The king who ruled Gaza with an iron fist since 2007 is Hamas. We will pray that Hamas loses its rule in Gaza. Israel's military is fully capable of doing this. The problem is the intense pressure from the international community, especially from the U.S., against Israel carrying out its mission. They talk about the necessity of Hamas being gone, but with their actions, they are tying Israel's hands.

"Ashkelon shall be uninhabited." South Ashkelon was forced to be vacated after October 7, because of the intense shelling by Hamas. Altogether, at the time of writing, half a million Israelis have been forced to leave their homes due to shelling from both Hamas in the South and Hezbollah in the North.

"A mixed people shall dwell in Ashdod." (Zec 9:6) Targum Jonathan is an ancient Aramaic paraphrase from the Second Temple Period, which was approved to be used in the synagogues for all who did not understand Hebrew. It reads like this, "A foreign nation, Israel, whom the Philistines mocked as foreigners, will dwell in Ashdod." Today, Ashdod is one of Israel's largest cities!

"... and I will cut off the pride of Philistia." Rabbi Ibn Ezra, who lived 900 years ago, comments on this as follows: "The pride of the Philistines will become extinguished since their city [Gaza] will be settled by Israelis." Gaza belongs to the Promised Land that God has given to Israel forever.

GOD'S WILL FOR GAZA

"I will take away its blood from its mouth, and its abominations from between its teeth; it too shall be a remnant for our God; it shall be like a clan in Judah, and Ekron shall be like the Jebusites." (Zec 9:7)

Now we have arrived at the most current and important verse in the chapter regarding the future of Gaza! This verse has enormous implications for the situation we are currently in, when the whole world holds its breath and wonders what will happen to all the Arabs in Gaza. The Bible has the answer!

The prophecy begins: "I will take away its blood from its mouth, and its abominations from between its teeth;" Rashi says: "This refers to the blood that they have shed." Ibn Ezra adds: "The Philistines drank the blood of those they murdered." This is definately a fitting description of Hamas' bloodthirsty terror that the whole world could witness on October 7.

I am reminded of a video report in which the wife of a Palestinian terrorist said, "We must kill the Jews in our land with our teeth. With our teeth we shall eat the Jews." It was not enough that Hamas carried out the horrific massacre that defies description on October 7. Moreover, thousands in Gaza celebrated this terrible death, terror, mutilation, and rape of defenseless women and children and the desecration of dead bodies, with rejoicing and fireworks in the streets. David wrote in his lament over the death of Saul and Jonathan: "Tell it not in Gath, publish it not in the streets of Ashkelon, lest the daughters of the Philistines rejoice, lest the daughters of the uncircumcised exult." (2 Sam 1:20) This is exactly what took place everywhere in Gaza on October 7.

But, here in Zechariah, God says in this 2,500-year-old prophecy, that he will come to put an end to this terror in Gaza. May it be soon!

"... it too shall be a remnant for our God; it shall be like a clan in Judah, and Ekron shall be like the Jebusites." What a mighty prophecy which will surely shake the world when it comes true! Ibn Ezra comments on this verse as follows: "The Philistines will cease their abominable habit of drinking the blood from the victims that they have murdered, **for they will now follow the true God** ... only Philistines who want to serve the true God will be left." Also Radak states: "for God will destroy the wicked among them ... **The Philistines will be the most prominent in Judah in their service to God.**"

This is how Rashi comments on this verse: "Amphitheaters and circuses will be used by the princes of Judah to teach the Torah [the Word of God]." Can we imagine that the Word of God will be preached in the "Palestine Square" in Gaza City where Hamas held its mass meetings and displayed its rockets and jihad terrorists in the fight against Israel? What a vision of the future!

In the summer of 1991, I traveled with my family and three other families from Sweden to Moscow to pray in the Red Square. The communists still had power over the former Soviet Union and we left there on a mission from the Lord to pray on the Red Square that it would be opened for the Gospel, so that revival meetings could be held there. By God's guidance, we all, including our children, marched six times around the square and prayed silently for this, while the state police (the KGB) carefully watched every step we took. The seventh time around, we knew that we should not pray, but simply praise God as we walked around the square. How could that happen without attracting the attention of the KGB?

To our big surprise—just then—someone let go of a large balloon up in the sky above the Red Square. So we could walk around the square, look up to the sky with our hands raised and praise God without attracting any attention. Everyone else in the square was looking to the sky and pointing. When we had finished marching, we stopped and read chapter 18 in the Book of Revelation about the judgment of the harlot. It was a sunny, cloudless summer day. We had just finished reading the chapter, when suddenly there was thunder from a clear blue sky over the square. God gave his affirmation! Within a few years, the first evangelist came and preached the Gospel in a big revival meeting on the infamous Red Square in Moscow! God is powerful and able to do the same miracle in Gaza. Hallelujah!

It says: "… and the people of Ekron shall be like the Jebusites." Ibn Ezra and Radak comment on this: "The inhabitants of Ekron [the Philistines] will show respect for Israel just as the Jebusites served Israel in the time of King David." And Rashi: "Ekron [Gaza] will be full of study halls [for the Word of God]," and of "pure-hearted men" (Rabbi David Altschuler, 1687–1769), "just like Jerusalem" which was originally a Jebusite city (Rashi).

Elie Mischel, an orthodox rabbi in Israel today, comments on this: "Zechariah says that the Philistine cities of Gaza will turn into Jewish cities, just as Jerusalem did. There will come a day when the streets of Gaza City will not be used to train terrorists, but rather be like 'a study hall in Judah'."[45]

A MARVELOUS FUTURE FOR ISRAEL

The powerful prophecy in Zechariah 9 then turns to Israel: "Then I will encamp at my house as a guard, so that none shall march to and fro; no oppressor shall again march over them, for now I see with my own eyes." (Zec 9:8)

My "house" is primarily talking about the Temple in Jerusalem, but it can also mean the land of Israel, which the Lord also calls "My land." (Joel 3:2) The Lord says that he will protect his land "against opressors and against those who march to and fro." On October 7, 3,000 Hamas terrorists suddenly crossed the border into Israel to murder, torture, mutilate and rape. They came and went as they pleased, back and forth across the border with their hostages. The Lord says that this will not be repeated. Israel will again live in safety, just as in the prophetic dream. It says, "no oppressor shall again march over them, for now I see with my own eyes." On October 7, God turned his eyes away from Israel for a moment.

---

45 Elie Mischel, "A Prophecy for our Time: Zechariah 9 and the Gaza War", *Israel365 News*, Nov 6, 2023, *https://israel365news.com/378529/a-prophecy-for-our-time-zechariah-9-and-the-gaza-war* [Dec 22, 2023].

Afterwards there follows a powerful messianic prophecy:

"Rejoice greatly, O daughter of Zion! Shout aloud, O daughter of Jerusalem! Behold, your king is coming to you; righteous and having salvation is he, humble and mounted on a donkey, on a colt, the foal of a donkey. I will cut off the chariot from Ephraim and the war horse from Jerusalem; and the battle bow shall be cut off, and he shall speak peace to the nations; his rule shall be from sea to sea, and from the River to the ends of the earth." (Zec 9:9-10)

This prophecy about the Messiah was fulfilled partly when Jesus rode into Jerusalem before His last Passover, as it says:

"Now when they drew near to Jerusalem and came to Bethphage, to the Mount of Olives, then Jesus sent two disciples, saying to them, 'Go into the village in front of you, and immediately you will find a donkey tied, and a colt with her. Untie them and bring them to me. If anyone says anything to you, you shall say, 'The Lord needs them,' and he will send them at once.This took place to fulfill what was spoken by the prophet, saying, Say to the daughter of Zion, 'Behold, your king is coming to you, humble, and mounted on a donkey, on a colt, the foal of a beast of burden.'" (Matt 21:1–5)

However, the entire messianic prophecy was not fulfilled on this occasion. The concluding part is saved for the return of Jesus, when all wars will cease and the promised Messiah of Israel will come to sit on his father David's throne in Jerusalem to rule over all peoples. "I will eradicate chariots from Ephraim and horses from Jerusalem. The bows of battle shall be cut off, and **he shall speak peace to the heathen. His dominion shall reach from sea to sea, and from the River to the ends of the earth.**" Isaiah prophesies the same thing about the

Messiah: "He shall judge between the nations, and shall decide disputes for many peoples; and they shall beat their swords into plowshares, and their spears into pruning hooks; nation shall not lift up sword against nation, neither shall they learn war anymore." (Isa 2:4) This is what we are waiting for to come true when Jesus returns, as He said: "... from now on you will see the Son of Man seated at the right hand of Power and coming on the clouds of heaven." (Matt 26:64)

Jesus is the Prince of Peace and the answer to the suffering of the Arabs in Gaza. He is the road to freedom both for Gaza and Israel. I am reminded of the well-known song by Andrae' Crouch "Jesus is the answer, for the world today. Above him there's no other, Jesus is the way." Jesus, he is the answer for our world today!

ISRAEL'S DELIVERANCE BY THE BLOOD OF THE COVENANT

"As for you also, because of the blood of my covenant with you, I will set your prisoners free from the waterless pit. Return to your stronghold, O prisoners of hope; today I declare that I will restore to you double." (Zec 9:11–12)

Hamas took over 240 innocent prisoners from Israel as hostages into Gaza. It is amazing how appropriate these verses are in their situation right now as this is being written, where they are sitting like prisoners in holes in the Hamas' tunnels in Gaza, deep down in the ground. May the Lord deliver them!

Israel is described in these verses literally as "prisoners of hope." God has entered into an eternal covenant with them. Paul writes about his countrymen according to the flesh that they have both the covenants and the promises (Rom 9:4). God's promises will never fail. Jesus has sealed them with His own blood.

"For I tell you that Christ became a servant to the circumcised to show God's truthfulness, in order to confirm the promises given to the patriarchs." (Rom 15:8) God will not let down his own people no matter what the enemy does. He will ultimately give them double for all their sufferings.

> "A Song of Ascents. When the LORD restored the fortunes of Zion, we were like those who dream. Then our mouth was filled with laughter, and our tongue with shouts of joy; then they said among the nations, 'The LORD has done great things for them.' The LORD has done great things for us; we are glad. Restore our fortunes, O LORD, like streams in the Negeb! Those who sow in tears shall reap with shouts of joy! He who goes out weeping, bearing the seed for sowing, shall come home with shouts of joy, bringing his sheaves with him." (Ps 126)

This Psalm is quoted by all Jews during Grace After Meals on every Sabbath and festival. God will restore Israel. They are the prisoners of hope.

The Arabs of Gaza also have hope. Jesus died for the whole world. Paul continues in Romans 15, "... and in order that the Gentiles might glorify God for his mercy. As it is written, 'Therefore I will praise you among the Gentiles, and sing to your name.'" (Rom 15:9) God also loves the Arabs in Gaza. Through the Messiah, they too have a wonderful future. Not without Israel, however, but together with them. "And again it is said, 'Rejoice, O Gentiles, **with** his people.'" (Rom 15:10) "This mystery is that the Gentiles are fellow heirs, members of the same body, and partakers of the promise in Christ Jesus through the gospel." (Eph 3:6)

"For I have bent Judah as my bow; I have made Ephraim its arrow. **I will stir up your sons, O Zion**, against your sons, O Greece, and wield you like a warrior's sword." (Zec 9:13)

This verse speaks of a spiritual awakening in Israel in connection with the war in Gaza, just as in the prophetic dream: "I will stir up your sons, O Zion, against your sons, O Greece, and wield you like a warrior's sword." Greece represents Hellenism and lawlessness, as opposed to Zion, God's holy mountain, and faithfulness to the Torah, the law. "For out of Zion shall go forth the law, and the word of the LORD from Jerusalem." (Is 2:3) It is this awakening we are now beginning to see in Israel in connection with the war in Gaza. Rabbi Elie Mischel writes:

"In recent weeks, tens of thousands of 'secular' Israeli soldiers have requested tzitzit, the tassels Jews are commanded to wear on the corners of their garments. Thousands of videos are circulating of Israeli soldiers of all religious backgrounds praying intensely before heading into battle."[46]

Rabbi Mischel continues:

"One of the great tragedies of our generation is the loss of so many young Jews to secularism and woke progressivism. Most young Jews in America and across the world were raised with little Jewish education and almost no connection to their glorious heritage. But since October 7th, many of these young Jews have begun to rediscover their heritage and to take pride in being Jews. Shocked by the rabid pro-Hamas antisemites that have taken over American universities and scream for the destruction of Israel, they now realize that they have been betrayed by their fellow woke activists. Though many young Jews continue to cling to secularism, a great Jewish awakening has begun."[47]

---

46 Ibid.

47 Ibid.

THE CONFLICT WITH YEMEN AND IN THE WEST BANK

"Then the LORD will appear over them, and his arrow will go forth like lightning; the Lord GOD will sound the trumpet and will march forth in the whirlwinds of the south." (Zec 9:14)

"... his arrow will go forth like lightning." Metzudos (Rabbi David Altschuler of Prague, 1687–1769) translated this, "His arrow will be sent out quickly like lightning against the enemy." Rashi comments, "God will go out and storm the people of the south [i.e. Yemen]." South and Yemen are the same word in Hebrew. The people of the South are thus Yemen.

This is a very strange verse in this particular context. After October 7, the Huthi rebels in Yemen, who are controlled by Iran, also began to threaten Israel. On October 31, for the first time, they sent an advanced Iranian-made ballistic missile against Israel. Israel then activated its new and most advanced air defense system and shot down the missile. The remarkable thing is that this air defense system is called "Arrow." It matches Metzudo's translation of this verse literally: "His arrow will be sent as quickly as lightning out against the enemy." Everone could witness exactly this on the Internet, October 31, 2023.

There is another very strange detail in the prophecy in Zechariah 9 that fits today's war in Israel. The concluding verses of the chapter read:

"The LORD of hosts will protect them, and they shall devour, and tread down the sling stones, and they shall drink and roar as if drunk with wine, and be full like a bowl, drenched like the corners of the altar. On that day the LORD their God will save them, as the flock of his people; for like the jewels of a crown they shall shine on his land. For how great is his goodness, and how great his beauty! Grain shall make the young men flourish, and new wine the young women." (Zec 9:15-17)

These verses primarily apply to those who are usually referred to as "settlers" in Judea and Samaria. This area that the media calls the "West Bank," is called the "Mountains of Israel" in the Bible. In Ezekiel, it is written about these settlers:

> "And you became the talk and evil gossip of the people, therefore, O mountains of Israel, hear the word of the Lord GOD: ... Thus says the Lord GOD: 'Behold, I have spoken in my jealous wrath, because you have suffered the reproach of the nations. Therefore thus says the Lord GOD: I swear that the nations that are all around you shall themselves suffer reproach. But you, O mountains of Israel, shall shoot forth your branches and yield your fruit to my people Israel, for they will soon come home." (Eze 36:3-4, 6-8)

In Zechariah 9, it says in verse 15: "The LORD of hosts will protect them." This is a strong promise to all the settlers in Judea and Samaria where many women and children are alone during the war in Gaza, because their husbands are drafted into the army and they are surrounded by hostile Arab villages. The risk that Hamas supporters will try to invade these settlements to carry out massacres similar to those that took place on October 7 is imminent. In this verse, the Lord God of hosts promises to protect them.

Then the prophecy continues, "and they shall devour, and tread down the sling stones." In recent decades the whole world has been able to see young Palestinian Arabs throwing stones at especially the Jews who live on the Mountains of Israel, in Judea, Samaria, and the eastern part of Jerusalem. They have become something of a symbol for the Palestinian terror in these areas. Multitudes of Jews have been injured for life by these stones and several have lost their lives.

In the end, the brave Jews on the Mountains of Israel, whom the whole world mocks and slanders, will triumph over this terror as well. They shall devour their enemies, and tread down the sling stones. Glory to God! "On that day the LORD their God will save them, as the flock of his people; for like the jewels of a crown they shall shine on his land. For how great is his goodness, and how great his beauty! Grain shall make the young men flourish, and new wine the young women." (Zec 9:16–17)

What a wonderful future for Israel—the prisoners of hope! God will keep his covenant with them and fulfill all his promises. They are jewels in a crown, shining on his land.

> "Behold, I will bring to it health and healing, and I will heal them and reveal to them abundance of prosperity and security. I will restore the fortunes of Judah and the fortunes of Israel, and rebuild them as they were at first. I will cleanse them from all the guilt of their sin against me, and I will forgive all the guilt of their sin and rebellion against me. And this city shall be to me a name of joy, a praise and a glory before all the nations of the earth who shall hear of all the good that I do for them. They shall fear and tremble because of all the good and all the prosperity I provide for it." (Jer 33:6–9)

> "Behold, I will gather them from all the countries to which I drove them in my anger and my wrath and in great indignation. I will bring them back to this place, and I will make them dwell in safety. And they shall be my people, and I will be their God. I will give them one heart and one way, that they may fear me forever, for their own good and the good of their children after them. I will make with them an everlasting covenant, that I will not turn away from doing good to them. And I will put the fear of me in their hearts, that they may not turn from me. I will rejoice in doing them

good, and I will plant them in this land in faithfulness, with all my heart and all my soul. For thus says the LORD: Just as I have brought all this great disaster upon this people, so I will bring upon them all the good that I promise them." (Jer 32:37–42)

"For if their rejection means the reconciliation of the world, what will their acceptance mean but life from the dead?" (Rom 11:15)

APPENDIX I: HOW CAN CHRISTIANS PRAY IN A WAR WHERE PEOPLE ARE KILLED?

By John Enarson

When war rages in Israel, I think many Christians feel confused and overwhelmed. Does being pro-Israel mean being against Arabs? How can Christians pray in a war where people are killed? If that is you, consider this important truth: **true love and grace for Arabs in the Middle East does not mean compromising on truth.** The God of the Bible does not do that. Grace and truth go together, always.

I love and have compassion for the Arab peoples caught in an ideology of death, lies, and violence. My biblically mandated love does not, however, require that I accept a false premise of a "Palestinian" national people. It is a convenient fiction which Arabs themselves (like PLO leader Zahir Muhsein) have admitted was very recently invented to fight Jewish independence in Israel.

It is true that we need to have God's heart toward, and pray for, the Arab enemies of Israel. But, too often it is coupled with a penchant for bartering away the truth in the name of misguided compassion.

A LEGITIMATE SWORD?

Consider some of these biblical truths. God takes no pleasure in the death of the wicked, rather that he should turn from his way and live (Eze 18:23). It stands to reason, if a murderer does not turn from his murderous attempts, he might also not live. "Rulers are not a terror to good conduct, but to bad. Would you have no fear of the one who is in authority? Then do what is good, and you will receive his approval, for he is God's servant for your good. But if you do wrong, be afraid, for **he does not bear the sword in vain. For he is the servant of God, an avenger who carries out God's wrath on the wrongdoer**" (Rom 13:3–4).

There is much debate over this well-known passage. All the same, it does say that legitimate authorities do not "bear the sword in vain." Turning the other cheek applies when someone personally insults you, but it does not biblically extend to legitimate judges and rulers of a society. That would make a mockery of justice.

I am reminded of the Christian intercessor Rees Howells. He faced similar questions and chose to lead his Bible school in deep prayer for the Allies throughout the war. He did not permit those praying to sleep any more than soldiers on the front. He took it on as a personal obligation to defeat Hitler himself in prayer. I believe Howells made the right choice.

PACIFISM IN BIBLICAL CONTEXT

Christian pacifism has a long history which I will not address here. Suffice it to say that it is based on replacement theology (supersessionism) which attempts to interpret only the New Testament as normative, while in some sense relegating the Hebrew Bible (the "Old Testament") as something old, passé, and not normative. Interpreting 25% of the Bible, while in some sense disregarding 75%, should be the definition of taking something out of context.

And Christian pacifism does not work. Even the heroic pastor and martyr, Dietrich Bonhoeffer, who was inspired by Gandhi and WWI to become a committed pacifist, felt morally compelled to partake in the assassination attempt against Hitler!

If you struggle with ideas of pacifism, you may want to consider different sides of the issue in "The Morality of War," *Moral Choices: An Introduction to Ethics* by Scott B. Rae (Grand Rapids: Zondervan, 2009).

TRADING AWAY ISRAEL

If you are not grounded in the truth of Scripture and history, it is easy to feel overwhelmed with complexity. Whenever actual conflict resurges, the airwaves immediately begin a bombardment with subtle deceptions and animosity toward Israel—the world's only Jewish state. Times of open conflict make it even that much harder for anyone to listen to the truth.

Some Evangelical organisations in the Middle East even find the whole issue of Israel to be a "stumbling block" for the gospel. They effectively try to trade away Israel to win more Arabs for Jesus. The results are few and produce some of the most anti-Zionist Christians you will ever meet.

God will not grant a great harvest in the Arab world to an Israel-hating, replacement-theology "gospel." It is also a betrayal of those Arab Christians who under great threat and persecution stand for God's Word and truth regarding Israel. We personally know of a few who can never go public or else they risk losing their lives.

HAMAS NEEDS TO MEET THE GOD OF ISRAEL

Too many Arabs are steeped and trapped in indoctrinating lies from childhood. The answer is not to compromise with untruths in the name of misguided emotional compassion. It may also require miraculous signs for many to be set free. The Six-Day War was a severe blow to jihadist faith in the Middle East. Islamism was deeply shaken, but it revived after the Iranian Revolution in 1979, when Khomeini said they lost to the Zionists only because they were too backslidden. Muslims must recommit.

Any future losses in today's Middle East cannot be explained away so easily. Hamas needs to see the fact that the God of Israel supernaturally fights for Israel. Pray that this truth will set more people free. Psalm 83 says, "Cover their faces with shame, LORD, so that they will seek your name...Let them know that you, whose name is the LORD—that you alone are the Most High over all the earth" (Ps 83).

PRAYING FOR MILITARY VICTORY?

A wise Jewish proverb says, we should pray for miracles, but not rely on them. During the war, I sent Christian intercessors the official "Prayer for the State of Israel" and the "Prayer for Israel's Defense Forces," including prayers for granting Israel military "victory." But many Christians feel they can only pray generally for peace, and hope for the best. Maybe it will just go away soon and all violence will stop. At most, they pray for God to strike the enemy with "confusion," and hope the rockets miraculously end up in the sea.

That might happen. But praying for the IDF to have wisdom and victory in stopping jihadists from killing both innocent Jews and Arabs, may legitimately entail that those jihadists die. That is not unbiblical to pray for. The key is that it saves other innocent victims from dying and going to their graves. This may even extend to innocent bystanders who die in war.

As Naftali Bennet once put it bluntly on *Al Jazeera*: by turning a private home into a rocket launcher, it is the same as if Hamas effectively murdered those innocents too. If it is necessary in order to protect innocent lives, **including undo risk to the soldiers' own lives**, it is the justified obligation of a nation to kill such murdering jihadists if they refuse to stop their killings.

According to the British Col. Richard Kemp, Israel has done more than anyone **in the history of warfare** to protect the rights of civilians in a combat zone. Israel often drops non-explosive "roof knocking" devices, constantly drops leaflets, and even makes personal phone calls to residents, well in advance of hitting a sensitive target! Any further resulting deaths are squarely on the heads of the jihadists. That blood will require a reckoning from Hamas on Judgment Day.

THE DEATH TOLL

Some observers wonder how the number of casualties can be so skewed. This is either a disturbing way of asking why more Jews can't just die, or it is moral confusion. A battle between good and evil is not somehow supposed to be an "even fight." The reason the casualty number in Israel is tragic, but low, is because Israel does everything it can to keep it low. The reason the death toll in Gaza is also tragic, but so low, is because Israel (not Hamas) does everything it can to keep it that low. Israel has the full capability of wiping out all of Gaza. But they don't, because they don't want to hurt anyone unnecessarily.

One should also keep in mind that most death tolls reported by the media, or the UN, are generally just taking Hamas' own "honourable" word for it. This, coupled with the well-documented phenomenon of "Pallywood"—staging tragedy, photo ops, and funerals—effectively render Gaza death tolls wild guesses in the dark.

Israel has good values, independent democratic institutions, and a free press to keep it honest. Hamas and the PLO's relationship with the truth is simply absurd. It doesn't even factor in.

PRAY LIKE NEVER BEFORE

Pray for the Arabs in Israel, in Gaza, in Lebanon, in Jaffa, in Ramallah, in Nablus, in Bethlehem, in Hebron, in all the Middle East. Pray that those jihadists who try to murder the innocent are stopped. Pray that truth will prevail and deliver those who are trapped in lies and darkness. Pray that God would comfort the terrified children in the conflict, that he will have mercy upon them, and grant that the Muslim children would not grow up to absorb the deceptions of society.

Pray Psalm 83, that the jihadist spirit will be humiliated and that many will see that the LORD God of Israel is the true and living God, who will not allow Israel, His "firstborn son," to be destroyed. Pray that the IDF wins a swift victory such that as few as possible suffer.

Pray that the love and truth of the gospel would pierce the darkness. Pray for those brave Arab believers who already stand with the truth in God's word regarding Israel. Pray that God will send out many more into the harvest field of the Middle East who preach a full Gospel, including God's unchanging faithfulness toward Israel.

Official Prayer for the State of Israel

"Our Father in Heaven, Israel's Rock and Redeemer, bless the State of Israel, the first flowering of our redemption. Shield it under the wings of Your loving kindness and spread over it the Tabernacle of Your peace. Send Your light and truth to its leaders, ministers and counselors, and direct them with good counsel before You.

"Strengthen the hands of the defenders of our Holy Land; grant them deliverance, our God, and crown them with the crown of victory. Grant peace in the land and everlasting joy to its inhabitants.

"As for our brothers, the whole house of Israel, remember them in all the lands of their dispersion, and swiftly lead them upright to Zion Your city, and Jerusalem Your dwelling place, as is written in the Torah of Moses Your servant:

"'Even if you are scattered to the furthermost lands under the heavens, from there the LORD your God will gather you and take you back. The LORD your God will bring you to the land your ancestors possessed and you will possess it; and He will make you more prosperous and numerous than your ancestors. Then the LORD your God will open up your heart and the heart of your descendants, to love the LORD your God with all your heart and with all your soul, that you may live' (Deut. 30).

"Unite our hearts to love and revere Your name and observe all the words of Your Torah, and swiftly send us your righteous Messiah of the house of David, to redeem those who long for Your salvation. Appear in Your glorious majesty over all the dwellers on earth, and let all who breathe declare: The LORD God of Israel is King and His kingship has dominion over all. Amen, Selah."[48]

Official Prayer for the Israel Defence Forces
"May He who blessed our fathers, Abraham, Isaac, and Jacob, bless the members of Israel's Defense Forces and its security services who stand guard over our land and the cities of our God from the Lebanese border to the Egyptian desert, from the Mediterranean Sea to the approach of the Aravah, and wherever else they are, on land, in air and at sea. May the LORD make the enemies who rise against us be struck down before them. May the Holy One, blessed be He, protect and deliver them from all trouble and distress, affliction and illness, and send blessing and success to all the work of their hands. May He subdue our enemies under them and crown them with deliverance and victory. And may there be fulfilled in them the verse, 'It is the LORD your God who goes with you to fight for you against your enemies, to deliver you' (Deut. 20). And let us say: Amen."[49]

---

48 From the traditional Jewish prayer book; translation from *The Koren Shalem Siddur: Nusah Ashkenaz* (Jerusalem: Koren Publishers Jerusalem Ltd., 2017) 522.

49 Ibid.

APPENDIX II: CHARTERS OF DEATH

"When people criticize Zionists, they mean Jews. You're talking anti-Semitism." *—Dr. Martin Luther King, Harvard University, 1968*

THE HAMAS CHARTER

From the Covenant of the "Islamic Resistance Movement" (i.e. Hamas).[50]

In The Name Of The Most Merciful Allah

"Ye are the best nation that hath been raised up unto mankind ..." ([The Quran], "Al-Imran," verses 109–111)

"Israel will exist and will continue to exist until Islam will obliterate it, just as it obliterated others before it" (The Martyr, Imam Hassan al-Banna,[51] of blessed memory).

---

50 "Hamas Covenant 1988", *The Avalon Project* (Yale Law School), *https://avalon.law.yale.edu/20th_century/hamas.asp* [Dec 22, 2023].

51 Hassan al-Banna was the founder of the Muslim Brotherhood in Egypt in the 1920s. Hamas claim affiliation with that movement.

Introduction

... Our struggle against the Jews is very great and very serious. It needs all sincere efforts. It is a step that inevitably should be followed by other steps. The Movement is but one squadron that should be supported by more and more squadrons from this vast Arab and Islamic world, until the enemy is vanquished and Allah's victory is realised.

Article 2

The Islamic Resistance Movement is one of the wings of Moslem Brotherhood in Palestine. Moslem Brotherhood Movement is a universal organization which constitutes the largest Islamic movement in modern times. ...

Article 6

The Islamic Resistance Movement is a distinguished Palestinian movement, whose allegiance is to Allah, and whose way of life is Islam. It strives to raise the banner of Allah over every inch of Palestine ... In the absence of Islam, strife will be rife, oppression spreads, evil prevails and schisms and wars will break out. ...

Article 7

As a result of the fact that those Moslems who adhere to the ways of the Islamic Resistance Movement spread all over the world, rally support for it and its stands, strive towards enhancing its struggle, the Movement is a universal one.

The Islamic Resistance Movement is one of the links in the chain of the struggle against the Zionist invaders. ... The Prophet, Allah bless him and grant him salvation, has said:

> "The Day of Judgement will not come about until Moslems fight the Jews (killing the Jews), when the Jew will hide behind stones and trees. The stones and trees will say O Mos-

lems, O Abdulla, there is a Jew behind me, come and kill him. Only the Gharkad tree would not do that because it is one of the trees of the Jews" (*related by al-Bukhari and Moslem*).[52]

Article 8

Allah is its target, the Prophet is its model, the Quran its constitution: Jihad is its path and death for the sake of Allah is the loftiest of its wishes.

Article 9

As for the objectives ... from its mosques would the voice of the mu'azen emerge declaring the establishment of the state of Islam ...

Article 11

The Islamic Resistance Movement believes that the land of Palestine is an Islamic *Waqf* consecrated for future Moslem generations until Judgement Day. It, or any part of it, should not be squandered: it, or any part of it, should not be given up. Neither a single Arab country nor all Arab countries, neither any king or president, nor all the kings and presidents, neither any organization nor all of them, be they Palestinian or Arab, possess the right to do that. Palestine is an Islamic *Waqf* land consecrated for Moslem generations until Judgement Day. This being so, who could claim to have the right to represent Moslem generations till Judgement Day?

---

52 *Bukhari* and *Muslim* are the authors to the two most authoritative and generally accepted collections of *hadith* (traditions of the Prophet). This tradition (*hadith*), attributed to the Prophet, has been frequently quoted in Islamic literature, ancient and modern. The Egyptian troops who launched the assault on the Bar-Lev Line in the Yom Kippur War of 1973, were equipped with "booklets of guidance" which included, inter alia, this same quotation.

This is the law governing the land of Palestine in the Islamic *Sharia* (law) and the same goes for any land the Moslems have conquered by force, because during the times of (Islamic) conquests, the Moslems consecrated these lands to Moslem generations till the Day of Judgement. ...

Article 12

Nationalism [*Wataniyya*], from the point of view of the Islamic Resistance Movement, is part of the religious creed. Nothing in nationalism is more significant or deeper than in the case when an enemy should tread Moslem land. Resisting and quelling the enemy become the individual duty of every Moslem, male or female.[53] A woman can go out to fight the enemy without her husband's permission, and so does the slave: without his master's permission.

Nothing of the sort is to be found in any other regime. This is an undisputed fact. If other nationalist movements are connected with materialistic, human or regional causes, nationalism of the Islamic Resistance Movement has all these elements as well as the more important elements that give it soul and life. It is connected to the source of spirit and the granter of life, hoisting in the sky of the homeland the heavenly banner that joins earth and heaven with a strong bond. ...

Article 13

Initiatives, and so-called peaceful solutions and international conferences, are in contradiction to the principles of the Islamic Resistance Movement. Abusing any part of Palestine is abuse directed against part of religion. Nationalism of the Islamic Resistance Movement is

---

53 *Fard 'ayn*, is an individual duty under Islamic law, to distinguish from *fard ki-faya*, which is a collective duty. *Fard 'ayn* is an absolute duty which overrides other considerations such as the duties of a wife towards her husband and of a slave towards his master.

part of its religion. Its members have been fed on that. For the sake of hoisting the banner of Allah over their homeland they fight. "Allah will be prominent, but most people do not know." ...

There is no solution for the Palestinian question except through Jihad. Initiatives, proposals and international conferences are all a waste of time and vain endeavors. The Palestinian people know better than to consent to having their future, rights and fate toyed with. As in said in the honourable *Hadith*:

> "The people of Syria are Allah's lash in His land. He wreaks His vengeance through them against whomsoever He wishes among His slaves. It is unthinkable that those who are double-faced among them should prosper over the faithful. They will certainly die out of grief and desperation."

Article 14

The question of the liberation of Palestine is bound to three circles: the Palestinian circle, the Arab circle and the Islamic circle. Each of these circles has its role in the struggle against Zionism. Each has its duties, and it is a horrible mistake and a sign of deep ignorance to overlook any of these circles. ...

Since this is the case, liberation of Palestine is then an individual duty for every Moslem wherever he may be.[54]

Article 15

The day that enemies usurp part of Moslem land, Jihad becomes the individual duty of every Moslem. In face of the Jews' usurpation of Palestine, it is compulsory that the banner of Jihad be raised. To do this requires the diffusion of Islamic consciousness among the masses, both on the regional, Arab and Islamic levels. It is necessary to

---

54 *Fard 'ayn,* cf. the note above.

instill the spirit of Jihad in the heart of the nation so that they would confront the enemies and join the ranks of the fighters. ...

It is necessary to instill in the minds of the Moslem generations that the Palestinian problem is a religious problem, and should be dealt with on this basis. ...

Article 16
It is necessary to follow Islamic orientation in educating the Islamic generations in our region by teaching the religious duties, comprehensive study of the Quran, the study of the Prophet's *Sunna* (his sayings and doings),[55] and learning about Islamic history and heritage from their authentic sources. ...

Article 17
The Moslem woman has a role no less important than that of the moslem man in the battle of liberation. She is the maker of men. Her role in guiding and educating the new generations is great. ...

Article 20
In their Nazi treatment, the Jews made no exception for women or children. Their policy of striking fear in the heart is meant for all. ...

Article 22
For a long time, the enemies have been planning, skillfully and with precision ... They were behind the French Revolution, the Communist revolution and most of the revolutions we heard and hear about, here and there. With their money they formed secret societies, such as Freemasons, Rotary Clubs, the Lions and others in different parts of

---

55 Relying on the Quran and the *Sunna* (tradition of the Prophet) is characteristic of fundamentalist Islamic movements, which hold the other three of the five sources of Sharia law in low esteem, namely: *Qiyas* (analogy), *Ijma'* (consensus) and *Ada* (local custom).

the world for the purpose of sabotaging societies and achieving Zionist interests. With their money they were able to control imperialistic countries and instigate them to colonize many countries in order to enable them to exploit their resources and spread corruption there.

You may speak as much as you want about regional and world wars. They were behind World War I, when they were able to destroy the Islamic Caliphate,[56] making financial gains and controlling resources. They obtained the Balfour Declaration,[57] formed the League of Nations through which they could rule the world. They were behind World War II, through which they made huge financial gains by trading in armaments, and paved the way for the establishment of their state. It was they who instigated the replacement of the League of Nations with the United Nations and the Security Council to enable them to rule the world through them. There is no war going on anywhere, without having their finger in it. ...

Article 27
Secularism completely contradicts religious ideology. Attitudes, conduct and decisions stem from ideologies. That is why, with all our appreciation for The Palestinian Liberation Organization [PLO]—and what it can develop into—and without belittling its role in the Arab-Israeli conflict, we are unable to exchange the present or future Islamic Palestine with the secular idea. The Islamic nature of Palestine is part of our religion and whoever takes his religion lightly is a loser.

Article 28
The Zionist invasion is a vicious invasion. ...

---

56 The breakdown of the Ottoman Empire signaled the end on the Caliphate.

57 The famous letter from Lord Balfour, the British Foreign Secretary, dated November 2, 1917, in which he pledged Britain's help in establishing a Jewish homeland in Palestine, which was to be given as a mandate (a mission) to the British to accomplish after the war.

Arab countries surrounding Israel are asked to open their borders before the fighters from among the Arab and Islamic nations so that they could consolidate their efforts with those of their Moslem brethren in Palestine.

As for the other Arab and Islamic countries, they are asked to facilitate the movement of the fighters from and to it, and this is the least thing they could do.

We should not forget to remind every Moslem that when the Jews conquered the Holy City in 1967, they stood on the threshold of the Aqsa Mosque and proclaimed that "Mohammed is dead, and his descendants are all women."[58]

Israel, Judaism and Jews challenge Islam and the Moslem people. "May the cowards never sleep."

Article 30
Jihad is not confined to the carrying of arms and the confrontation of the enemy. The effective word, the good article, the useful book, support and solidarity—together with the presence of sincere purpose for the hoisting of Allah's banner higher and higher—all these are elements of the Jihad for Allah's sake.

"Whosoever mobilises a fighter for the sake of Allah is himself a fighter. Whosoever supports the relatives of a fighter, he himself is a fighter." (*related by al-Bukhari, Moslem, Abu-Dawood and al-Tarmadhi*).

---

58 It is impossible to ascertain what this claim is based on. There is a popular Arabic song which denigrated those who failed to rear sons and only left behind daughters.

Article 31

The Islamic Resistance Movement is a humanistic movement. It takes care of human rights and is guided by Islamic tolerance when dealing with the followers of other religions. It does not antagonize anyone of them except if it is antagonized by it or stands in its way to hamper its moves and waste its efforts.

Under the wing of Islam, it is possible for the followers of the three religions—Islam, Christianity and Judaism—to coexist in peace and quiet with each other. Peace and quiet would not be possible except under the wing of Islam. Past and present history are the best witness to that.

It is the duty of the followers of other religions to stop disputing the sovereignty of Islam in this region ...

The Zionist Nazi activities against our people will not last for long. "For the state of injustice lasts but one day, while the state of justice lasts till Doomsday." ...

Article 32

World Zionism, together with imperialistic powers, try through a studied plan and an intelligent strategy to remove one Arab state after another from the circle of struggle against Zionism, in order to have it finally face the Palestinian people only. Egypt was, to a great extent, removed from the circle of the struggle, through the treacherous Camp David Agreement. They are trying to draw other Arab countries into similar agreements and to bring them outside the circle of struggle.

The Islamic Resistance Movement ["Hamas"] calls on Arab and Islamic nations to take up the line of serious and persevering action to prevent the success of this horrendous plan, to warn the people of the danger eminating from leaving the circle of struggle against Zionism.

Today it is Palestine, tomorrow it will be one country or another. The Zionist plan is limitless. After Palestine, the Zionists aspire to expand from the Nile to the Euphrates. When they will have digested the region they overtook, they will aspire to further expansion, and so on. Their plan is embodied in *The Protocols of the Elders of Zion,* and their present conduct is the best proof of what we are saying.

Leaving the circle of struggle with Zionism is high treason, and cursed be he who does that. "for whoso shall turn his back unto them on that day, unless he turneth aside to fight, or retreateth to another party of the faithful, shall draw on himself the indignation of Allah, and his abode shall be hell; an ill journey shall it be thither." ([*The Quran*] "The Spoils," verse 16). There is no way out except by concentrating all powers and energies to face this Nazi, vicious Tatar invasion. The alternative is loss of one's country, the dispersion of citizens, the spread of vice on earth and the destruction of religious values. Let every person know that he is responsible before Allah, for "the doer of the slightest good deed is rewarded in like, and the doer of the slightest evil deed is also rewarded in like."

The Islamic Resistance Movement consider itself to be the spearhead of the circle of struggle with world Zionism and a step on the road. The Movement adds its efforts to the efforts of all those who are active in the Palestinian arena. Arab and Islamic Peoples should augment by further steps on their part; Islamic groupings all over the Arab world should also do the same, since all of these are the best-equipped for the future role in the fight with the warmongering Jews.[59]

"..and we have put enmity and hatred between them, until the day of resurrection. So often as they shall kindle a fire of war, Allah shall extinguish it; and they shall set their minds to act corruptly in the

---

59 Despite their protestation to the contrary, Hamas uses Jews and Zionism interchangeably.

earth, but Allah loveth not the corrupt doers." ([*The Quran*] "The Table," verse 64).[60]

Article 33

The Islamic Resistance Movement, being based on the common coordinated and interdependent conceptions of the laws of the universe, and flowing in the stream of destiny in confronting and fighting the enemies in defence of the Moslems and Islamic civilization and sacred sites, the first among which is the Aqsa Mosque ... till Allah's purpose is achieved when ranks will close up, fighters join other fighters and masses everywhere in the Islamic world will come forward in response to the call of duty while loudly proclaiming: Hail to Jihad. Their cry will reach the heavens and will go on being resounded until liberation is achieved, the invaders vanquished and Allah's victory comes about.

Article 34

Palestine is the navel of the globe and the crossroad of the continents. Since the dawn of history, it has been the target of expansionists. The Prophet, Allah bless him and grant him salvation, had himself pointed to this fact in the noble *Hadith* in which he called on his honourable companion, Ma'adh ben-Jabal, saying:

> "O Ma'ath, Allah throw open before you, when I am gone, Syria, from Al-Arish to the Euphrates. Its men, women and slaves will stay firmly there till the Day of Judgement. Whoever of you should choose one of the Syrian shores, or the Holy Land, he will be in constant struggle till the Day of Judgement."

---

60 This verse explicitly talks about the Jews in its first part which is not quoted here.

Article 35

The Islamic Resistance Movement views seriously the defeat of the Crusaders at the hands of Salah ed-Din al-Ayyubi and the rescuing of Palestine from their hands, as well as the defeat of the Tatars at Ein Galot,[61] breaking their power at the hands of Qataz[62] and Al-Dhaher Bivers and saving the Arab world from the Tatar onslaught which aimed at the destruction of every meaning of human civilization. The Movement draws lessons and examples from all this. The present Zionist onslaught has also been preceded by Crusading raids from the West and other Tatar raids from the East. Just as the Moslems faced those raids and planned fighting and defeating them, they should be able to confront the Zionist invasion and defeat it. This is indeed no problem for the Almighty Allah, provided that the intentions are pure, the determination is true and that Moslems have benefited from past experiences, rid themselves of the effects of [Western] ideological invasion and followed the customs of their ancestors.

Article 36

While paving its way, the Islamic Resistance Movement, emphasizes time and again to all the sons of our people, to the Arab and Islamic nations, that it does not seek personal fame, material gain, or social prominence. It does not aim to compete against any one from among our people, or take his place. Nothing of the sort at all. It will not act against any of the sons of Moslems or those who are peaceful towards it from among non-Moslems, be they here or anywhere else. It will only serve as a support for all groupings and organizations operating against the Zionist enemy and its lackeys. ...

---

61 The battle of Ein Galot (1260) is the one that arrested the advance of the Mongols in the Middle East when they were defeated by the Muslim Mameluks under Baibars (1223–1277).

62 A Mameluke king of Egypt (1259–1260).

The last of our prayers will be praise to Allah, the Master of the Universe.

THE PLO CHARTER

The PLO (Palestine Liberation Organization) is the "peaceful" organization that the whole world, including the United States, wants Israel to make peace with, in order to have "two states living side by side in peace." Almost all of the articles in their Covenant explicitly or implicitly deny Israel's right to exist and reject any peaceful solution to the Arab-Israeli conflict. For example:

Article 9:
"Armed struggle is the only way to liberate Palestine."[63]

Article 15:
"The liberation of Palestine ... aims at the elimination of Zionism in Palestine ..."

Article 19:
"The partition of Palestine in 1947 and the establishment of the state of Israel are entirely illegal, regardless of the passage of time ..."

Article 22:
"... the liberation of Palestine will destroy the Zionist and imperialist presence and will contribute to the establishment of peace in the Middle East ..."

---

63 Aaron Lerner, "PA Schoolbooks and the PLO Charter," July 28, 1998, http:// gamla.org.il/english/article/1998/july/ler3.htm [June 9, 2011]; cf. "The Palestinian National Charter: Resolutions of the Palestine National Council July 1–17, 1968," *The Avalon Project* (Yale Law School), *https://avalon.law.yale.edu/20th_century/plocov.asp* [Dec 22, 2023].

The Constitution also denies the existence of the Jewish people as a nation and any ties it may have with the Land of Israel.

Article 20:
"Judaism, being a religion, is not an independent nationality. Nor do Jews constitute a single nation with an identity of its own."

The final conclusion of the Palestinian National Charter requires the annihilation of the State of Israel. As a condition for peace, Yasser Arafat promised to change the statute to say that the PLO accepts Israel's right to exist. To this day, it has not happened.

Despite the fact that the Palestinian National Council (PNC) made two formal decisions to revise the Palestinian National Charter (1996 and 1998) that call for the annihilation of Israel, this has never been implemented. PNC Chairman Salim Za'anoun instead claimed on February 3, 2001 in the Palestinian Authority's official newspaper, that the PLO Charter remained unchanged and is still in force.[64] Since then, the PLO Charter has never been questioned by the international community.

THE HEZBOLLAH CHARTER

One of Iran's first projects after the Islamic revolution in 1979 was to form the terrorist organization Hezbollah in Lebanon. It was Hezbollah that was the first to use suicide terrorists. From having started as a small and insignificant minority movement, after 44 years, it has taken over all of Lebanon.

Excerpt from the Hizbollah Program of 1985:[65]

---

64 Al-Hayat Al-Jadida (Feb 3, 2001), translated by MEMRI.

65 "The Hizballah Program," *The Jerusalem Quarterly* 48 (Fall 1988), http://zion ism-israel.com/hdoc/Hezbollah_Charter.htm [June 9, 2011].

"We see in Israel the vanguard of the United States in our Islamic world. It is the hated enemy that must be fought until the hated ones get what they deserve. This enemy is the greatest danger to our future generations and to the destiny of our lands, particularly as it glorifies the ideas of settlement and expansion, initiated in Palestine, and yearning outward to the extension of the Great Israel, from the Euphrates to the Nile.

"Our primary assumption in our fight against Israel states that the Zionist entity is aggressive from its inception, and built on lands wrested from their owners, at the expense of the rights of the Muslim people. Therefore our struggle will end only when this entity is obliterated. We recognize no treaty with it, no cease fire, and no peace agreements, whether separate or consolidated.

"We vigorously condemn all plans for negotiation with Israel, and regard all negotiators as enemies, for the reason that such negotiation is nothing but the recognition of the legitimacy of the Zionist occupation of Palestine. Therefore we oppose and reject the Camp David Agreements, the proposals of King Fahd, the Fez and Reagan plan, Brezhnev's and the French-Egyptian proposals, and all other programs that include the recognition (even the implied recognition) of the Zionist entity [Israel]."

APPENDIX III: THE MUSLIM BROTHERHOOD

The Muslim Brotherhood, regarded as the largest Islamist movement in the world today, was founded by Hasan al-Banna in 1928 and dedicated to the credo, "Allah is our objective. The Prophet is our leader. Qur'an is our law. Jihad is our way. Dying in the way of Allah is our highest hope."

In November 2001, a document called "The Project" was found during a raid by Swiss authorities in a luxury villa in Campione, Switzerland. The target of the raid was Youssef Nada, director of the Al-Taqwa Bank of Lugano, who has had active association with the Muslim Brotherhood for more than 50 years and who admitted to being one of the organization's international leaders. Among the documents seized during the raid was a 14-page plan written in Arabic and **dated 1 December 1982**, which outlines **a 12-point strategy "Towards a Worldwide Strategy for Islamic Policy"—identified as "The Project."** According to Nada's testimony to Swiss authoreties,

"Islamic scholars" with connection to the Muslim the Brotherhood had produced the unsigned document.[66]

Below is a list of tactics and techniques for an Islamic conquest of the West found in "The Project." They include:

- Making the Palestinian cause a global wedge issue for Muslims.

- Adopting the total liberation of Palestine from Israel and the creation of an Islamic state as a keystone in the plan for global Islamic domination.

- Instigating a constant campaign to incite hatred by Muslims against Jews and rejecting any discussions of conciliation or coexistence with them.

- Actively creating jihad terror cells within Palestine.

- Linking the terrorist activities in Palestine with the global terror movement.

- Collecting sufficient funds to indefinitely perpetuate and support jihad around the world.

---

66 Cf. Rachel Ehrenfeld, "The Muslim Brotherhood Evolution: An Overview," *American Foreign Policy Interests* (2011, 33:2, 69–85), *https://www.tandfonline. com/doi/abs/10.1080/10803920.2011.571059* [Dec 22, 2023]. Rachel Ehrenfel aquired a complete translation from Swiss authoreties and maintains that Yousef al-Qaradawi wrote "The Project: Towards a Worldwide Strategy for Islamic Policy." Cf. also Patrick Poole, "The Muslim Brotherhood 'Project," *Front-Page Magazine*, May 11, 2006, *http://frontpagemag.com/articles/Read. aspx?GUID={61829F93-7A81-4654-A2E8-F0A5E6DD3DC4}* [Sep 8, 2007].

Five year later, Hamas was created by the Muslim Brotherhood in 1987. Around the same time Al Qaida was also formed. Prime Minister Erdogan's political party in Turkey is founded on similar ideology as the Muslim Brotherhood. Before becoming Prime Minister, Erdogan was sentenced to 4 months in prison for quoting in public a poem with the following words, "The mosques are our barracks, the domes our helmets, the minarets our bayonets, and the faithful our soldiers."[67] Erdogan has made a political career in Turkey that is very similar to what Hitler's was in Germany.

The Muslim Brotherhood has declared that their goal is to take over the entire world for Islam out from Gaza. Turkey's Prime Minister Receep Erdogan has thrown his entire weight behind Hamas' Islamic world strategy.

LEADERS WITH DISCERNMENT

One of the few European politicians who has managed to discern this strategy is José Maria Aznar, who was Prime Minister of Spain from 1996 to 2004. Aznar has launched an organization called *Friends of Israel*, consisting mainly of non-Jewish Europeans and Americans, including the the former president of Peru, Alejandro Toledo and John Bolton, the former UN ambassador from the United States.[68]

At the launching of his organization Aznar stated,

> "Anger over Gaza is a distraction. We cannot forget that Israel is the West's best ally in a turbulent region. For far too long now it has been unfashionable in Europe to speak up for Israel. In the wake of the recent incident on board a ship

---

67   *BBC News*, Nov 4, 2002.

68   "Many Prominent Europeans Launch Pro-Israel Initiative," *OneJerusalem*, June 19, 2010, *http://onejerusalem.org/2010/06/many-prominent-europeans-launc. php* [9-5-2011]; cf. *http://friendsofisraelinitiative.org* [Dec 22, 2023].

full of anti-Israeli activists in the Mediterranean, it is hard to think of a more unpopular cause to champion.

"Uniquely in the West, [Israel] is the only democracy whose very existence has been questioned since its inception. In the first instance, it was attacked by its neighbors using the conventional weapons of war. Then it faced terrorism culminating in wave after wave of suicide attacks. Now, at the behest of radical Islamists and their sympathizers, it faces a campaign of delegitimization through international law and diplomacy.

"Sixty-two years after its creation, Israel is still fighting for its very survival. Punished with missiles raining from north and south, threatened with destruction by an Iran aiming to acquire nuclear weapons and pressed upon by friend and foe, Israel, it seems, is never to have a moment's peace.

"The real threats to regional stability ... are to be found in the rise of a radical Islamism which sees Israel's destruction as the fulfillment of its religious destiny ... Israel is our first line of defense in a turbulent region ... If Israel goes down, we all go down. To defend Israel's right to exist in peace, within secure borders, requires a degree of moral and strategic clarity that too often seems to have disappeared in Europe. The United States shows worrying signs of heading in the same direction.

"The West is going through a period of confusion over the shape of the world's future. To a great extent, this confusion is caused by a kind of masochistic self-doubt over our own identity; by the rule of political correctness; by a multiculturalism that forces us to our knees before others; and by a secularism which, irony of ironies, blinds us even when we are confronted by jihadists promoting the most fanatical incarnation of their faith. To abandon Israel to its fate, at this moment of all moments, would merely serve to illustrate how far we have sunk and how inexorable our decline now appears.

"For Western countries to side with those who question Israel's legitimacy, for them to play games in international bodies with Israel's vital security issues, for them to appease those who oppose Western values rather than robustly to stand up in defense of those values, is not only a grave moral mistake, but a strategic error of the first magnitude."[69]

---

69 "Former Spanish President Stands Up For Israel," *OneJerusalem*, June 17, 2010, *http://onejerusalem.org/2010/06/former-spanish-president-stand.php* [Sep 5, 2011].

ABOUT THE AUTHOR

Lars Enarson, a native of Sweden, is the founder and president of *The Watchman International*, a ministry dedicated to "prepare the way for Messiah." A major part of his ministry is *Nordic 7:14*, a grassroots prayer movement of Bible-believing Christians, crying out for revival in northern Europe and back to Jerusalem.

Lars has been in full time ministry since the early 1970s. His passion is to see a restoration in our day of the original, apostolic gospel from Jerusalem.

Lars resides with his wife Harriet and family in Israel, where he produces TV-programs and Video Prayer Alerts, with prophetic insights, reports, and specific prayer points about the present situation in the Middle East. He is the author of several books and a Bible teacher who travels extensively throughout the world.

For more information, visit his website *larsenarson.com*.